Recipes *for* Roughing It Easy

DIAN THOMAS

Recipes *for* Roughing It Easy

Great Outdoor Recipes for the Backwoods and Backyard

THE DIAN THOMAS COMPANY
SALT LAKE CITY, UTAH
www.dianthomas.com

Distributed by Betterway Books,
an imprint of F&W Publications, Inc.,
1507 Dana Avenue,
Cincinnati, OH 45207.
www.fwpublications.com
(800) 289-0963

05 04 03 02 01 5 4 3 2 1

Thomas, Dian
Recipes for Roughing It Easy: Unique recipes for outdoor cooking and backyard grilling plus many great ideas for creative outdoor fun; with step-by-step instructions for each activity./Dian Thomas

Includes index
ISBN 0-9621257-8-4
1. Camping   2. Cooking   I. Title

Acknowledgments

Many talented people contributed to the preparation of this book. For their "indoor" and "outdoor" skills, I would like to thank Brighton Girls Camp, John Barraclough, Carolyn Campbell, Dwane Cude, Barbara and Jack Dahl, Julie Goldstein, Barbara Harris, Noel Hilden, Rebecca Hobbs, Carole Houtz, Dianne T. King, Jayne Malan, Ed Micu, Victoria Nicholson, Guida Ponte, Erin Simmons, Cameron Thomas, Cherie Thomas, Clyde Thomas, Daniel Thomas, Rebekah Thomas, Brian Twede and Fiona Willis.

Special thanks for the complete, easy-to-use references that have made writing recipes and editing cookbooks so much more interesting and enjoyable.

The New Food Lover's Companion by Sharon Tyler Herbst, Barron's © 2001. Anyone interested in food or anything about it should not be without this book.

The Recipe Writer's Handbook by Barbara Gibbs Ostman and Jane L. Baker, Wiley © 2001. Recipe writing is simplified, with explicit directions given.

Table of Contents

About the Recipes

My first book, *Roughing It Easy*, was written over 25 years ago. Over the years I have had many requests for outdoor recipe ideas. In answer to these numerous requests, *Recipes for Roughing It Easy* was conceived and born.

These recipes were developed and tested in the hope that your outdoor adventure would also give you an introduction to new cuisines. Many recipes are "trendy" for today, such as the Italian focaccia bread that also serves as the crust for pizza, a yeast bread to accompany meals or the base of a recipe such as the pizzelle. Others may use unfamiliar terms which I have attempted to explain. Some may use a foreign method, which I have also tried to cover in the recipe instructions.

Two of my employees, both with French cooking experience, helped to develop new recipes. New terms for old familiar ingredients used in their recipes have been defined to share with you ideas from an international cuisine.

The Dutch oven is the equipment backbone of outdoor cooking, so Dutch oven cooking directions are included with most recipes. Some recipes also offer information about cooking on the upside-down lid or creating an oven by placing hot coals both underneath the oven and on the top of its lid.

Grilling is a cooking technique familiar to almost everyone. Simple grilling is enhanced by a variety of grills and even some "homemade" grills for the backyard, including the tin can stove, wheelbarrow and wagon grills and the flowerpot grill. Camp stoves and their fuel varieties are covered in detail, and most recipes tested on the camp stove can be prepared in your own kitchen at home. A variety of camp stoves were used for recipe testing.

Stick and foil cooking ideas are limitless. I've just scratched the surface. This book will inspire you to come up with your own. And don't overlook the entertaining novelty ideas.

Enjoy your outdoor cooking adventures by trying many of the new and delicious recipe combinations from everyday to gourmet plus a few all-time "signatures," including Kick-the-Can Ice Cream.

Dedication

This book is respectfully dedicated to the original Brighton Girls' Camp, my favorite mountain playground and my first outdoor kitchen, which was destroyed by fire January 19, 1963.

To Dianne T. King, in gratitude for more than 25 years of dedicated service and support.

And to Barbara Harris, for inestimable contributions to the creation of this book.

My Roughing It Easy Life

My fondness for outdoor cooking, which has always been vivid in my memory, began when I was a very young child. My father was a forest ranger in the Manti-La Sal National Forest in the mountains of southern Utah. I loved to accompany him when he took our family to the wilderness for outings and recreation.

My first taste of outdoor cooking was my dad's homemade sourdough biscuits. Both of my grandfathers raised sheep and lived in sheepherder's wagons. My dad's outdoor cooking followed his father's example, which included baking sourdough biscuits in a Dutch oven. As the biscuits were cooking—and I'm certain they reached at least four inches in height—I remember the fragrant, heavenly scent as steam came wafting out of the oven. I would slather a hot biscuit with butter and honey. Then I would barely need to chew as the delicious biscuit melted in

Real-life Roughing It: Grandfather's sheep wagon at Wolf Creek Pass

my mouth. I fell in love with outdoor cooking at that moment.

Outdoor recreation has always been my priority. I have continued to learn as much as I could about having fun outside.

When I was twelve, our family moved to Salt Lake City, site of the 2002 Winter Olympic Games. As a transplant, I felt lost in the big city. But that summer I attended Brighton Girls' Camp, nestled in a pine-filled mountain valley of the Wasatch Mountains, and I knew I had arrived home.

After my first summer experience at Brighton, I wanted to return to the camp as a staff member. I began by working in the

I began Roughing It at Brighton Girls' Camp

camp kitchen as a cook's assistant for two years, then as a counselor for two years, and then as program director for a year. At age 21, I became the camp director and was responsible for hiring and training staff and developing activities for the camp. Ten one-week programs were held each summer for 150 girls each week. As a counselor and camp director, my goal was always to be open to new ideas, activities and recipes. I believe that my early pursuit of limitless variety was a seed that led to my moniker, "first lady of creativity."

After my camp director days, I traveled as a professional speaker with Brigham Young University (BYU) in Provo, Utah, sharing my enthusiasm for outdoor cooking throughout the USA and Canada. I continued to pursue my enthusiasm by teaching both indoor and outdoor cooking classes.

All four of my brothers were Scouts, and I've enjoyed participating in outdoor cooking and recreation with the Scouting program for many years. One of the highlights of my association with the Boy Scouts came when I was asked to judge the outdoor cooking contest for the National Boy Scout Jamboree in Pennsylvania. I've been able to communicate my love for the outdoors to Scouts nationally by writing articles for *Scouting*.

On the cover of Scouting *Magazine*

Roughing It with Boy Scouts as judge of the National Jamboree Cooking Contest

As I continued to share my creative ideas, I also relished the unique cuisines of all 50 states and over 40 foreign countries. I even visited Hawaii to learn specifically about pit cooking. I stayed up all night to watch the Hawaiians dig the pit, build the fire and cook the pig for a traditional luau.

My outdoor curriculum thesis was rewritten as my first book, *Roughing It Easy*. After I appeared on the *Tonight Show* with Johnny Carson, the book soared to the top of the New York Times best-seller list as nationwide audiences embraced my ideas. Over a million copies of *Roughing It Easy* were sold, thanks to the national publicity. After three years, my classroom audience moved to screen viewers via television.

During the next fifteen years, I appeared as a regular family member on NBC's *Today Show* and ABC's *Home Show* and *Good Morning America*. I literally came "out of the woods" to teach outdoor cooking to celebrities such as Tom Brokaw, Jane Pauley, Bryant Gumbel, Regis Philbin, Willard Scott, Joan Lunden and even President and Mrs.

Roughing It indoors with Johnny Carson, The Tonight Show

Reagan. Along with well-known TV personalities, I continued to share my ideas with outdoor enthusiasts and their viewing audiences across the country.

Roughing It Easy *sells over a million copies to become a New York Times best-seller*

This new book, *Recipes for Roughing It Easy*, continues to encourage creativity in cooking and to promote outdoor fun with your family and friends. I invite you to savor life in the great outdoors and discover for yourself the joy of outdoor cooking.

I still love to cook outdoors. The food is wonderful, and the outdoor air enhances the flavor, fun and fellowship. Cooking outdoors sets a stage to share the wonders of nature with family and friends. By preparing enjoyable meals outside, you

My appearances on TV with (clockwise from top left) Tom Brokaw, Jane Pauley, Regis Philbin, Nancy & President Ronald Reagan, Willard Scott, Martin Short, Joan Lunden and Bryant Gumbel

will create memories that will long be remembered.

Besides encouraging a oneness with nature, outdoor cooking is a sensory experience. Rather than turning a dial to precisely 350°F., you use all *five* senses to monitor the cooking. You may **watch** as corn boils in a pot or hot dogs brown on a grill. You may **hear** a steak sizzle. You might **touch** the top of a Dutch oven cake or bread to **see** if it "feels" done. Feel the steam rise with the palm of your hand. Your sense of **smell** will help you delight in the full-bodied aroma of food as it cooks.

Recipes for Roughing It Easy offers over 200 recipes plus many ideas to make your outdoor adventure easy, fun and less stressful. The focus is on easy-to-use techniques and foods that are delicious and memorable. As recipes were tested, I realized that it is possible—and often fun—to prepare favorite recipes using a different cooking method each time. Techniques are provided for grilling, Dutch oven and Dutch oven lid cooking, gas stove cooking, and cooking at home. For additional ideas, consult www.dianthomas.com.

Bon appétit outdoors!

Dian Thomas

CHAPTER 1

Cooking and Camping Equipment

From many years of camping and outdoor cooking, I have learned that organization is the key to any successful event. There's nothing worse than being at a campsite and realizing you've forgotten something. After much trial and error, I developed an easy system with everything organized and at my fingertips.

Before I pack my Jeep, I have all basic equipment laid out as efficiently as possible. I use large plastic storage containers to hold everything and I label each for kitchen equipment, camping equipment, staples, etc. I always use detailed checklists, which I've shared (pages 214–215). A checklist will get you started with the basics you'll need to get organized and make your own outdoor cooking plans.

Preparing, cooking and eating food outdoors is relaxing and fun. Americans have enjoyed it for many generations. The fresh air, wood smoke flavoring, cool mornings and warm fire are uniquely satisfying and restorative. Food tastes especially delicious because its flavor is enriched by the clean, pollution-free air. Your spirit is renewed, your creativity is enhanced, and you gain a new perspective when cooking outside.

Plan Ahead to Enjoy the Outdoors

Cooking in an outdoor kitchen requires some specific skills that can be developed using a few basic facts and guidelines. The carefully tested methods of cooking and the delicious recipes in this book will give you ideas on how to add interest and variety to your outdoor adventure.

With advance planning, meals cooked outdoors can be more delicious and interesting than meals cooked at home. To plan your menu, consider tastes, methods of cooking, costs, length of the outdoor adventure, and the number and ages of people who will be eating. One way to plan convenient, practical meals for your outing is to first determine your activities, then decide which meals would best accompany those activities (see page 213 for One-Day Meal Planner.)

Select Proper Cooking Equipment

Your cooking area is a vital part of creating your outdoor experience. Selecting the right cooking equipment is the key to preparing delicious meals for an around-the-campfire dinner.

Consider the length of your stay and the accessibility of the area you plan to visit when deciding which cooking equipment to take along. When you drive, you'll probably take more equipment than you would to an area where hiking is required. An afternoon cookout will obviously require less equipment than a week's stay. An easy way to decide which cooking equipment is needed is to plan menus, then make an itemized equipment list (see 214 for a general camping equipment list).

Begin with Basic Utensils

Consider buying a lightweight stainless steel knife, fork and spoon combination that nests together. For your first outing, you may want a single frying pan and camp stove. As you continue to enjoy the outdoors and gain further experience, you'll want to add equipment gradually, such as one good pan, a Dutch oven and a grill. If you are dining with just two or three people, a 1- or 2-quart pot may be all you need. A stainless steel cup can serve many purposes; not only is it a drinking and measuring cup, it can also hold hot and cold foods such as cereals, soups, stews and puddings. When you're considering whether to add additional equipment, think simplicity and versatility. Use your imagination. You can devise many types of cooking equipment as needed from items such as sticks, aluminum foil, plastic self-sealing bags and tin cans.

- If you need to take water with you on a camping trip, you can carry it in plastic self-sealing bags placed inside the can for leakproof transportation to your destination. Before mixing food, line the can with a plastic self-sealing bag. Mix and serve the food; then discard the bag or rinse it out to reuse it.

- A smooth-sided tin can may be a rolling pin. (Do not use glass containers for this purpose.)

- A tuna fish can is a cookie or biscuit cutter when both ends are removed so that the air can pass through as you use it.

A #10-size tin can lined with a 1-gallon plastic self-sealing bag for serving food

- Cut out the sides and bottom of a plastic bleach bottle to create a homemade scoop.

- A 3-pound coffee can or #10-size can from restaurants makes a versatile utensil that can be used to cook in, to mix foods in, and to serve from . . . and it can be disposed of without a second thought. Recycle a potato flake can, a coffee can or other cans of this size to use in the outdoors.

- To cut down on the number of dirty pans, take along a large oven cooking bag and line a pot with the bag. This way, you can use the pot for more than one meal without washing it. Discard bag after using and reline with a new one.
- Heavy-duty aluminum foil can be shaped into a serving bowl. It can also be wrapped around a square made from a wire coat hanger to make a frying pan. Foil can be used to make a shallow pan deeper by building up taller sides.
- Plastic self-sealing bags are very handy for mixing food. Simply combine all ingredients, push most air out, seal, and squeeze until well mixed. To coat food before cooking, combine flour and seasonings in the bag, drop in pieces of meat or chicken, and toss. You can empty a box of muffin or cake mix into the bag. Cut instructions from the box and tape them to the outside. When you're ready to mix, add the liquid ingredients, squeeze air out of the bag, seal and mix by squeezing with your hands.
- A heavy-duty self-sealing bag can be used to crush cookies or crackers into crumbs or for crushing nuts with a can.
- A Frisbee can double as a serving tray for paper plates. Give each guest a different-colored Frisbee lined with a stack of paper plates to last for your entire outing. At the end of the meal, the top plate is peeled off and discarded. If youare serving a meal with more than one course, your guests can peel off a plate after each course.

Mealtime and fun time: paper plate-lined Frisbee

- Control insect problems by using an embroidery-hoop lid. Fasten a piece of plastic wrap between the two rings of an embroidery hoop as if it were a piece of fabric to be stitched. Place the hoop over a plate or bowl, and you will prevent flies and gnats from invading your dish, and the food will not dry out.

- Organize your tools and utensils by purchasing a hanging shoe or lingerie organizer with see-through pockets. The pockets are perfect for holding paper plates, napkins, cups and cooking and eating utensils. This hanging equipment bag is storable in a kitchen or utility closet, and transfers easily to an outdoor hook or tree branch when you are ready to cook outdoors. If a storm threatens your outing, your equipment stays dry within the compartments of the bag. Should you choose to move indoors or to another site, you can pack your cooking equipment in just minutes.

Embroidery hoop and plastic wrap lids protect food outdoors

Equipment bag for utensils and supplies

Basic Fire Equipment

A shovel, bucket of water and heatproof gloves are important fire-building accessories. Select a site at least 15 feet away from anything that might ignite. Be especially aware of overhanging branches. Brush the area to eliminate pine needles.

Cooking with Fire

If you could go back to the time of the explorers and early settlers, you would discover that a wood fire was the primary means of cooking and keeping warm.

Times have changed. Today, we love our many modern conveniences. A large segment of the population, however, still enjoys camping and cooking outdoors. With the innovations of new techniques and equipment, there is now a growing population who wants to camp and cook outdoors. In days of old, people were concerned about personal survival. Today, we are mindful of the survival of our environment. In many areas, open fires are against the law because of extreme fire hazards they pose. Be sure you know current restrictions before starting a fire or trekking in an unfamiliar area.

Preparation for Fire Cooking

There's no feeling quite like the cozy warmth of a campfire even on a hot day. Advance preparation and an understanding of fire safety rules will enhance your enjoyment and help you to safeguard the environment in wilderness areas. If your destination allows open fires, know the fire safety regulations. For campfire cooking techniques, *Roughing It Easy* thoroughly covers this subject with additional information on fire building. Many established campsites have built-in fire areas; however, some campground fire pits are housed in deep holes that are inconvenient for cooking. If the site you select does not have facilities for cooking, ask for permission to prepare a fire. Large fires are not required for cooking. Charcoal briquettes or hot coals from wood are most effective.

Millions of outdoor enthusiasts have responded to the ideas in Roughing It Easy

Tinder

Tinder is any burnable material smaller in size than your little finger. It is most helpful for starting a fire. Fine shavings, bark, dry pine needles, small twigs, dry leaves and dry grass would all be considered examples of tinder. You can create homemade tinder using the following method:

Egg carton tinder

An excellent tinder can be created with a cardboard egg carton, lint from your clothes dryer and wax. Fill the pockets of an empty cardboard (not styrofoam) egg carton with lint from your clothes dryer. Cotton balls can be used in place of dryer lint. Place the egg carton on a section of newspaper. Melt paraffin wax or old candles **in a double boiler** and pour wax into each lint pocket. When wax has hardened, break off a section of the egg carton every time you need a fire starter. Each section will burn for 10 to 15 minutes.

Egg carton fire starter

Waterproof Matches

To prepare for your outing, protect matches from exposure to moisture by dipping the match heads in paraffin or fingernail polish. After dipping, place inside the grooves of a piece of corrugated cardboard to dry or place the matches inside the grooves of cardboard in order to dip a group at the same time into melted paraffin. **Because wax has a very low combustion point, for safety reasons be sure to use a double boiler to melt the paraffin.**

Batteries and Steel Wool Fire Starter

An easy and dramatic way to start a fire is to use two flashlight batteries and a strip of grade 00 or finer steel wool. Cut or stretch a piece to about 8 inches in length. Align two good flashlight batteries on top of each other in an upright position (as if they were placed inside a flashlight). Hold one end of the steel wool strip against the bottom of the lower battery. **Carefully rub the other end of the steel wool across the "nub" of the upper battery.** As soon as the steel wool sparks, place it on tinder or other burnable material and slowly blow on it. As you blow, the flame will grow more intense. This method works very well for starting a fire in windy areas. For safety reasons, always pack the steel wool and batteries in separate containers.

Steel wool and batteries fire starter method

Camp Stove Cooking

For personal safety reasons and with respect for the environment, most recipes in this book call for camp stove, Dutch oven and grill cooking methods.

When World War I ended, cars were more affordable and many families took advantage of their newfound mobility to explore the great American outdoors. Fold-up camp stoves soon became traveling companions in car trunks and were found in vacation cabins, camping trailers and hunting lodges. Their popularity increases every year.

In choosing a camp stove for outdoor use, consider variables such as the kinds of foods selected, availability of water, number of people with you, distance you might have to carry supplies, climate conditions, terrain, and length of outing.

Stoves are often classified by the type of fuel they require.

The most common fuels are propane, butane (cartridge or cans) and white gas.

The following types of stoves are easy to carry and easy to use for the recipes in this book.

Camp Stoves

Camp stoves come with one, two or three burners. Light-weight stoves are equipped with one burner and weigh between one and two pounds. Using two or three burners is convenient for cooking more than one item or preparing food for a group. Three-burner stoves are ideal for breakfast, because you can place a griddle over two of the burners and use the third burner for heating beverages or preparing an additional recipe.

When purchasing your outdoor stove, consider one that comes with a wind-screen attachment. This is handy if the wind suddenly attempts to blow out the flame. Fuel for the stove varies from a can of pressurized fuel to liquid gas.

Two-Burner Stove

A two-burner stove will burn for approximately two hours per fuel canister with both burners on high. It may be designed to consume both automotive unleaded gasoline as well as liquid fuel. The two-burner stove is inexpensive to operate. It offers even heat distribution, deep flame ports on the sides for wind resistance, ease of lighting, an adjustable flame, and a nickel-chrome-plated steel rod grill for easy cleaning.

Two-burner camp stove with wind-shield

One-Burner Stove

The one-burner stove is excellent for general use except on a very windy day. Available from restaurant supply stores, it has the advantage of a butane cartridge, which is easy to change.

A one-burner camp stove

Grill/Griddle Stove

The grill/griddle stove is very convenient for a picnic or camping. Turn over the grill—and you have a griddle.

The camp grill/griddle

Fuels

Many types of fuels are available for your outdoor cooking experience. Fuel-burning appliances are for cooking as well as for providing a way to keep warm and a source of light. They vary in cost, convenience and performance. The most important criterion in selecting a fuel is to know how you will use the appliance. Will you be eating around a campfire at a national park? Or will you be hiking into remote high country? The following paragraphs describe the characteristics and advantages of several common fuels. With all of the fuel options available, you have many choices to meet specific outdoor needs.

Liquid Fuel or White Gas

Liquid fuel or white gas is relatively inexpensive and easy to find at sporting goods and variety stores. Its main advantages are heat output and economy. It is sold in one-gallon steel cans, so if you don't mind carrying a can to your outdoor destination, liquid fuel might be the right choice for you. Unlike butane and propane, this fuel burns hot, even at subzero temperatures.

While you don't have to dispose of the empty liquid fuel cans like you do the empty propane or butane cylinders, you do need to fill liquid fuel appliances and pump them occasionally.

Liquid fuel in a one-gallon can

Propane Fuel

This highly available and convenient fuel is used by more campers than others because it is so easy to use. Check to see if an adapter is needed, and simply attach the fuel cylinder to the adapter and begin cooking.

Propane is heavier in weight than other fuel options and weighs two to three pounds per cylinder. It is reliable but does operate less effectively at sub-freezing temperatures than liquid fuel. Cold weather creates a pressure drop in the cylinder, which decreases propane fuel output. While propane isn't the least expensive fuel option, if you plan to camp for several days or weeks, choosing to buy a refillable bulk tank will result in lower fuel costs.

Propane is available in small, convenient cylinders

Butane Fuel

This fuel source is very convenient and lightweight, and is available at many sporting goods and restaurant supply stores.

It may be the right choice if you are a backpacker who wants to travel light, because both the fuel itself and butane-fueled appliances weigh very little. Butane works best in fair weather. Subfreezing temperatures affect the pressure in the canister. Butane canisters are not recyclable.

Butane can be used for the backpacker's grill and more

Blended Fuel

Propane/butane blended fuel has a better performance in cold temperatures and high altitudes. It uses a liquid withdrawal system which ensures an optimum performance when cold. It is available in recyclable aluminum canisters.

Unleaded Gasoline Fuel

The main advantages are easy availability and low cost. With a price of one-tenth the cost of propane, unleaded gasoline is the least expensive of all fuel choices. It is available at every gas station. In an emergency, it's possible to siphon from your car or RV tank to use in a lantern or stove that is compatible with unleaded gasoline. Appliances will last longer if you select a more pure fuel (one of the above).

While unleaded gas generally has a stronger odor than camping fuel, there is no additional odor when the stove is operating. Both camping fuel and unleaded gasoline are flammable and should be used and stored properly. **Using unleaded gas in traditional gas stoves is not recommended except in emergency situations, because it will lessen performance and reduce generator life span.** Cooking with unleaded gas also requires special care. Do not fill the tank near the stove or indoors or near an open flame. Always clean up spills, and always follow the manufacturer's directions (see www.coleman.com).

Charcoal Briquette Fuel

These small pillow-shaped coals offer a dependable source of steady heat for outdoor cooking.

Interestingly, Henry Ford's versatile innovations include both the Model T Ford and charcoal briquettes. In the 1920s, while searching for a use for wood scraps left over after the production of his Model T's, he learned to convert them into charcoal and opened the Ford Charcoal plant. Henry Ford's relative, E. G. Kingsford, helped select the site for the plant, and the company was later renamed Kingsford's Charcoal Briquettes. Today, Kingsford still leads the United States in the manufacture of charcoal in this country and continues Henry Ford's tradition, annually converting more than one million tons of wood scraps into quality charcoal briquettes. Along with Kingsford Charcoal Briquettes, there are also many other brands from which to choose.

Grill Cooking

The mouth-watering aroma of meat sizzling on a grill brings to my mind memories of many wonderful canyon parties over the years. Outdoor cooking grills include backpacker grills, gas stove grills, hibachis, kettle grills, and open braziers as well as improvised grills—a child's wagon, metal garbage can lid, terra-cotta flower pot, tin can grill and wheelbarrow.

For grilling, the most common types use wire racks. The most versatile of this type has racks that raise or lower to regulate heat. Many are large enough to cook more than one item. You can also create your own grill using a cookie cooling rack. (Do not use a rack from a refrigerator.)

Hibachi

So small that you can grill on your patio, at the beach or in the woods, the hibachi (from Japan) is usually made from cast iron. It is heavy so you would probably not want to transport it by foot. It is available in various sizes to accommodate the amount of grilling space you need for the type of cooking you

The hibachi allows for easy outdoor grilling

have planned. Because of the hibachi's small grilling space, meals can only be prepared for a smaller number of people.

Kettle Grill

The round kettle grill barbecues large and small pieces of food. The smallest size grill is ideal for camping. With its lid on, it works like an oven. Without its lid, the grill can be used for lamb or pork chops, steaks, chicken, vegetables and hot dogs. Dampers on the top and bottom of the kettle grill regulate the amount of oxygen and can be opened or closed to adjust the grill's temperature.

The kettle grill is extremely versatile

The open brazier

Open Brazier

Suspended over a shallow bowl which holds the coals, the open brazier comes in several sizes, is lightweight and has wheels on the legs for portability. Look for one on which the grill can be moved up and down to regulate the heat. It is especially good for cooking flat pieces of meat such as hamburgers, fish, chicken and steaks.

Gas Stove Grill

A tabletop gas stove grill features an easy method of cooking and grilling at the same time. It also offers the versatility of a traditional grill with the combined convenience of a propane grill. This grill unit is perfect for meats such as hot

One-burner stove with grill

dogs, hamburgers, chicken and steaks and has a burner for frying eggs, boiling corn or additional frying or braising. Some grills have a griddle which can be added to interchange with the grill for frying pancakes, French toast, etc.

The gas stove grill is compact enough to take on outings and offers a versatile cooking surface for preparing most meals. It is easy to operate, the heat output is constant, and the grill stove will run up to four hours using a 16-ounce propane cylinder. The gas stove grill is a convenient, easy way to cook and grill at the same time.

Volcano Cook Stove

This new stove enables you to cook using a griddle, Dutch oven, grill or frying pan. Its unique design allows you to cook many different dishes at once using the Volcano as the main heat source. It has a top grill for barbecuing steaks, chicken, hamburgers, etc., and a bottom grill for briquettes.

This stove is equipped with a very efficient draft system which allows for easy temperature control. It is safe on a tabletop, tablecloth or wood deck, because the

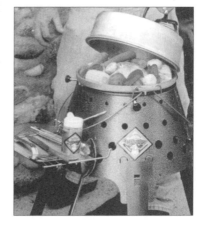

The Volcano outdoor cook stove

exterior and bottom of the stove generate very little heat. A model is available which uses either propane or charcoal briquettes. For ordering information, call 1-800-846-6355.

Improvised Grills

Many items in your home can be adapted to a grill. All you need is a permanent container such as metal, concrete, or terra-cotta. Fill the bottom with dirt or sand, cover with aluminum foil, add charcoal briquettes and place a rack on top.

Brick Grill

A simple outdoor grill can be created by using aluminum foil, bricks, charcoal briquettes and a grilling rack. Place a sheet of foil on the ground. Space two bricks far enough apart to support both edges of a grilling rack (near the outer foil edges).

A simple improvised grill using bricks, rack and charcoal briquettes

Arrange charcoal briquettes on the foil between the two bricks and light. Use a cookie cooling rack as the cooking surface. To adjust the temperature of your improvised grill, experiment using one or more bricks under the rack to adjust the height above the briquettes.

Tin Can Grill

An improvised, inexpensive grill can be made in just a few minutes. All that is needed is a #10-size can (a 3-pound coffee can), tin snips, aluminum foil and a pair of gloves. Beginning at the open end of the can, cut 2-inch-wide parallel slits down the side, to about 3 inches from the bottom, repeating around the can. Bend the strips away from the center of the can to form a low basketlike container. Fill the bottom of the can with dirt. Cover the dirt and strips with heavy-duty aluminum foil. You have now created an improvised tin can grill. Place the charcoal on top of the foil and lay the grilling rack on top of the metal strips. It is important to keep the distance between the grilling rack and the charcoal at about 3 to 4 inches. (Bend the strips to this distance.)

A bonus of this grill is that it can be discarded after one use, and replaced at very little cost. Individual stoves can be made by a group to involve more people in the fun.

A #10-size tin can will make an easy and economical grill

Use tin snips to cut two-inch strips down the sides of the can

Line the tin can with heavy-duty foil before adding charcoal

Add a rack, and you're ready to grill

Unique Improvised Grills

If you don't own a barbecue or if you are having a "dry run," enjoying a day at the beach, visiting a picnic area, or camping in your backyard, you might be happy with a child's wagon grill, wheelbarrow grill, a metal garbage can lid or even a terracotta flowerpot.

Wagon grill

The wagon or the wheelbarrow might tote your supplies to your site. Adapting it for grilling is as easy as filling the base with 6 inches of gravel, sand or dirt to insulate the bottom from the heat. Cover the dirt with extra-heavy-duty aluminum foil, to prevent coals from sinking into the dirt and insure that air will circulate. On top of the foil in the center make a pyramid of charcoal briquettes. Pour lighter fluid over the charcoal and light. Drape a pair of oven mitts over the wagon tongue or wheelbarrow handles so they'll be close by when needed.

Wheelbarrow grill

When briquettes are burning, arrange bricks around the outside edge, adapting them for the grill or rotisserie. If you simply want to do stick cooking, omit the bricks. The most efficient height for grilling is 3 to 4 inches above the coals.

Dirt can be stored between

Garbage can lid grill

Terra-cotta flowerpot grill

uses by covering the wheelbarrow or wagon with an old plastic tablecloth with Velcro stitched to seal the corners. Moisture will rust out the bottom of your wagon or wheelbarrow if it gets wet.

Backpacker's Grill

A backpacker's rack can be purchased from a sporting goods store. To use the backpacker's grill, place coals on the ground; the backpacker's rack sits on legs about 4 to 8 inches above. If the dirt is loose or sandy, assure uniform heat by placing a piece of heavy-duty aluminum foil over the dirt to keep the briquettes

The backpacker's grill is the easiest of all to set up and use

from settling into the sand and causing them to lose heat.

The heat for the backpacker's grill is very simple to regulate. To increase heat, simply push the rack toward the ground. To decrease heat, raise the rack farther from the coals.

Charcoal Briquette Lighting

The most common way to start charcoal briquettes is to stack them into a pyramid shape and cover with lighter fluid. Let the fluid-dampened briquettes rest for 3 or 4 minutes before lighting. Toss a lighted match onto the briquettes. After approximately 5 to 10 minutes, the fire will burn lower, but the charcoal will continue to heat. You will know that the briquettes are heating properly when white ash begins to form around the edges. Twenty to 40 minutes are needed before the briquettes are ready for cooking (approximately 70 percent ashed-over with a dull red glow). To test, see page 72. Time varies depending on the type of briquettes, the dose of lighter fluid and the amount of wind. Use caution when wearing flowing clothes and long, flyaway hair. When the briquettes are ready, use tongs to spread coals evenly over the cooking surface. Do not add more lighter fluid once the flame goes out, because it can cause flare-ups and burns. Never use alcohol, gasoline or kerosene to start briquettes.

Chimney Starter

A chimney starter is an excellent investment to help charcoal briquettes light faster. Crumple two full pages of newspaper into wadded balls and place in the bottom section of the starter. Pile briquettes in the top above the newspapers. Light the newspapers. A Frisbee or paper plate may be fanned near the opening to increase the circulation of air which helps briquettes to ignite. When briquettes have ash and flame, pour into the fire bed.

The chimney starter is an ideal way to light charcoal briquettes

Match Light Briquettes™

A predetermined amount of lighter fluid is added to Match Light Briquettes™ so they are ready to cook on in 10 to 15 minutes, depending on the number of briquettes used and weather conditions. Ignite by simply striking a match. Like traditional charcoal briquettes, Match Light Briquettes have an indefinite shelf life if closed tightly in the bag and stored in a dry place. When briquettes are moist, they will not light efficiently. Also, if the bag is left open or is torn, the solvent (lighter fluid with which Match Light Briquettes are treated) evaporates and can only be lit using additional lighter fluid.

Egg Carton Briquette Starter

Briquettes can also be lit by using the cardboard egg carton tinder described on page 13. Remove the lid from the egg carton tinder and set the base of the carton inside the lid. Set a charcoal briquette in each egg cup. Continue to pile briquettes onto the carton. Light the carton and wait for the briquettes to heat. Depending on the size of your fire, you may need to use only half of the egg carton.

Half an egg carton fire starter will start briquettes amazingly fast

Hair Dryer

If you are at home or in a place where electricity is available, a portable hair dryer can be used to blow hot air across the briquettes to speed igniting. They will glow with a light flame. The air from the dryer causes oxygen to spread throughout the briquettes in just moments. Always point the dryer in a direction away from yourself and others because sparks may blow out of the grill. Make sure that nothing flammable is nearby. Briquettes will heat in about 15 minutes. (If your hair dryer is made of plastic, keep it far enough from the flame so that it does not melt.)

A hair dryer speeds up the heating of hot coals

Bellows

Use fireplace bellows to blow air across the briquettes, which increases oxygen and speeds heating.

Frisbee or Paper Plate

If you don't have access to a hair dryer or bellows, fan the briquettes with a Frisbee or paper plate to increase oxygen circulation and speed heating.

Wood Chips

Wood chips add a nice smoky flavor to grilled foods. Soak the chips in water one hour and add a few to your hot coals. Using mesquite gives a sweet flavor contrasted with hickory, which is still sweet but less delicate. Other grilling woods are apple, cherry, maple, pecan, oak and walnut. Pine and spruce, which contain pitch, can ruin the flavor. A variety of wood chips can be purchased where grilling supplies are sold.

Grilling Temperature

To avoid undercooking or overcooking, consider cooking all foods to their optimum doneness by creating different temperatures on the grill. Divide your grill into three sections (or as many as needed) for "heat settings." For the highest temperature setting, arrange the briquettes so they are touching each other. Follow a checkerboard pattern of spacing in the second section for "medium" and finally, place briquettes a few inches apart in the third section to create the "low" setting.

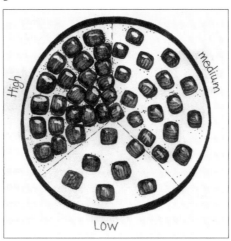

One grill with three temperature settings

Adding New Briquettes

When heated briquettes are burning out and you wish to add new ones for long cooking times, arrange them around the edge of the hot charcoal bed and gradually push them toward the center of the grill as they burn down.

Extinguishing Briquettes

To reuse briquettes that are not completely burned when cooking is finished, extinguish the briquettes by placing them into a can and covering with aluminum foil or a nonplastic lid to cut off the oxygen supply. With no oxygen, they cannot burn. In a kettle-type grill simply close the vent and put on the lid. Shelf life is indefinite. Store in a closed can in a dry place.

Safety Precautions

Charcoal briquette fumes give off toxic carbon monoxide when burning. Briquettes are never safe to use indoors, but are completely safe to use outside. **When using charcoal lighter fluid, never add new fluid once the briquettes are lit.**

Cooking Shirt

The "cooking shirt" is designed as a combination apron/pot holder for all of my outdoor cooking. It has a breast pocket to hold various items and is the best cover-up for keeping clothes clean. It's also a great way to recycle two old shirts into continued use. You will need:

**An old long-sleeved button-type shirt—
denim, chambray, flannel, etc.
An old long-sleeved sweatshirt**

1. Cut the sleeves off the button-type shirt a few inches below the elbow.
2. Cut the sleeves off the sweatshirt above the elbow, almost to the armpit.
3. Place cut edges of the shirt sleeve and sweatshirt sleeve, right sides together, and pin at the seam. (If both shirts are not the same distance around, see • on page 30.)
4. Pin right sides together. Sew a 5/8-inch seam joining shirts.

You now have an extra-long sweatshirt sleeve at the end of your button-type shirt. Push the sweatshirt sleeves down when cooking, draping them over your hands to lift hot pans and to protect from heat. The cooking shirt is also ideal for keeping your hands warm or roasting marshmallows on a cool evening around a campfire.

- Sometimes the circumference of the sweatshirt is larger than that of the shirt, so it must be made smaller. Either sew a new seam from the cuff to the cut edge of the sweatshirt, making it the same distance around, or gather by stitching 2 basting seams around the sweatshirt cut edge at 5/8-inch and 1/4-inch and ease together. Pin at each 1/2 and then 1/4 and sew a permanent seam at 5/8 inch. If you don't have these types of old shirts, visit the thrift store for a large selection.

Convenient cooking shirt with pot-holder sleeves

Meal Organization

Ask each person participating in the outing or camping trip to join in the meal preparation and cleanup. Consider dividing the group into three subgroups. Each subgroup could perform one of the following tasks: (1) table setting, (2) cooking or (3) cleanup. Subgroups will rotate for each meal until each person has had a chance to do each job.

Eating Area

If your eating location does not have picnic tables, select a flat, shady area. Spread a tarp or army poncho before the table-cloth because the ground may be damp.

Specialty Cookware

Cookware manufacturers have updated their product lines to include specialty items designed for the outdoor cook. Some of the innovations include a lightweight grill/griddle combination, percolator and even an outdoor pressure cooker (to speed up the cooking at high altitudes where cooking times need to be increased).

Outdoor pressure cooker

A recent innovation is hard-anodized cookware for the outdoors. Some nonstick finishes also require less fat or oils, making cleanup a breeze.

Unbreakable serving and eating utensils are now available to bring the ambience of fine dining outdoors. For example, indestructible glasses and stackable/packable china and flatware are available for outdoor use. See www.dianthomas.com.

Mealtime Cleanup

To help expedite cleanup following your outing, consider the following tips:

- Keep meals simple so pans to wash are few. When baking Dutch oven desserts with lots of sugar that "sticks," I use heavy-duty aluminum foil on the bottom of the oven. I also often mix and/or serve foods in a plastic self-sealing bag to help ease cleanup.
- Rinse all pots, utensils and dishes as soon as you are finished so foods will not stick.

- Wash the least dirty dishes first and work your way to the dirtiest dishes. This keeps the water clean for a longer period of time.
- If you plan to cook over an open fire, soaping the outside of all pans with liquid detergent or soap lather before cooking makes it easier to wash off the black residue later.

Soaping pots and pans used over an open fire makes cleaning easy

High-Altitude Cooking

High-altitude cooking increases the cooking time for liquids approximately 2°F. per 1,000 feet. In San Diego (sea level), water boils at 212°F. At Brighton, Utah (8,000 feet above sea level), water boils at 212°F. minus 16°F. or 196°F. Food takes longer to cook the higher you go. No adjustment is necessary for yeast-risen baked goods, but allowing batter to rise twice before the final pan rising develops a better flavor. Baking requires specific leavening adjustments. For information, consult high-altitude baking on the Internet or your local county extension agent.

Preserving the Environment

Recreation in the outdoors should meet your needs without changing the beauty or balance of nature. Plan to leave an area in better condition than you found it by leaving nothing but footprints and taking nothing but pictures.

Plan ahead so your favorite campsite will be your great-grand-children's favorite, too

Outdoor Comfort

Having a pure water supply and keeping clean while hiking or camping can be challenging. The following suggestions will help simplify your daily routine and help make outdoor living more convenient for you.

Drinking Water Purification

Keep a plastic self-sealing bag in your pocket. Should you find a source of clean water, fill the bag and add a water purification tablet. After you've finished drinking, zip the bag, fold it and return it to your pocket for the next use. Always purify water before drinking unless it comes from a treated source. Portable water purification devices can be purchased at sporting goods stores.

To chlorinate one gallon of water, add ten drops of liquid chlorine bleach. Stir the bleach into the water and allow it to rest for one hour or more. If the water remains cloudy, double the amount of bleach.

Biodegradable Soap

To preserve the pristine nature of the outdoor environment, whenever you wash yourself or your clothes, use biodegradable soap. Always wash far enough away from any lake or stream to prevent dirty wash water from flowing back into the natural water around you. Wet wipes are an excellent basic hygienic item for keeping face and hands clean.

Bleach Bottle Waterspout

To create this unique waterspout, select a plastic bleach bottle with an airtight lid. With a small nail, poke a hole in the front of the bottle near the bottom for the spout. Fill the bottle with water. To wash hands, unscrew the lid. Air from the top forces a small stream of water from the spout. If a larger water stream is preferred, poke a bigger hole in the bottle using a golf tee. Tie the golf tee to the bottle handle to use as a stopper.

To use the waterspout at your outing, tie a rope to the bottle handle and then tie the bottle to a tree branch at the desired height for hand washing.

Bleach bottle waterspout

You can also equip your waterspout with a bar of biodegradable soap in a nylon stocking and hang it from the handle of the jug. For fun, you may want to paint a face on the jug with the spout hole as the mouth.

Outdoor Dressing Room/Shower

For privacy and conven-ience purposes, you can easily create an outdoor dressing room or show-er from an umbrella and two lightweight fabric shower curtains. Select an umbrella with a hooked handle. Open up the umbrella and hang it upside down from a tree branch about six feet above the ground. If all nearby branches are too high, tie the umbrella to a branch with a piece of rope, so that it hangs at

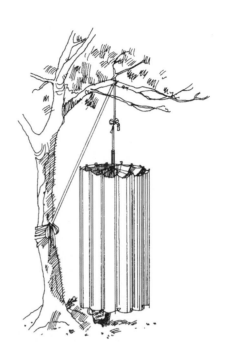

Privacy in the great outdoors

a six-foot level. Attach the holes at the top of the first shower curtain over the umbrella ribs. They are exactly the same dis-tance apart. After all the curtain holes on the first curtain are attached, repeat with the second shower curtain. Overlap the last two holes creating a door flap for dressing room/shower.

For shower water, select an unused new insecticide can filled with water. A dark one works best for setting in the sun to warm. This may also be placed where people wash their hands for a handy sprayer. When it gets very warm outside, fill it with cold water. Pump and spray the fine mist to cool off.

Note: This isn't cooking, but you might need a shower after sweating over hot coals!

Nighttime Bathroom Tissue Holder

This easy tissue paper and flashlight holder will help you both find your way in the dark and keep your tissue dry. Remove the cardboard tube from inside the center of a roll of bathroom tissue. Pull the paper out of the center of the roll, so that the roll itself doesn't rotate. Place the roll with a flashlight inside a plastic self-sealing bag. Pull tissue from the center of the roll so that it hangs outside the bag. Zip the bag partially closed. At night the flashlight inside the bag will shine through the clear plastic to help you find your way back to bed.

Take along a flashlight!

CHAPTER 2

Stick Cooking

Almost everyone's first experience with outdoor cooking began with sticks to roast marshmallows or hot dogs. Many a child has struck the Statue of Liberty pose with a flaming marshmallow as the torch. Thankfully, stick cooking has evolved to include simple and delicious meals suitable for outdoors.

One of my personal favorite campfire treats is the roasted cinnamon-sugar **Apple Pie on a Stick** (page 48). It is so easy—and simply delicious, too. Equipment for stick cooking is readily available—roasting sticks, wooden dowels, pitchforks, and, of course, actual sticks found anywhere outdoors; all can be used over an open fire or hot coals. Use your creativity and you'll discover the satisfaction of stick cooking for your favorite outdoor food.

Sticks were very likely the first cooking utensils. It's possible that cavemen and women actually roasted woolly mammoth steaks on sticks. Today when we recall happy memories of outdoor cooking, our thoughts usually return to stick cooking. We all remember roasting a hot dog or toasting a marshmallow above glowing embers (or maybe even in the coals) until it caught fire.

Everyone enjoys easy end-of-the-stick cooking

Stick cooking is easy, fast, convenient and versatile. It is similar to cooking on the broiler of a kitchen range where dry heat cooks the food.

Skewers and Sticks

Assorted skewers and sticks are available for outdoor cooking. Commercial metal sticks can be cleaned easily by putting them in the coals to burn off the drippings after use. Allow metal skewers to cool before reusing. Cooking sticks can be created from wooden dowels. Simply sharpen one end with a pencil sharpener or pocketknife. Before using bamboo or wooden skewers or sticks, it's a good idea to soak them first in water for several hours so that they will not burn. Always cook over hot coals rather than in direct flames when using a stick.

Two Types of Stick Cooking

A limitless variety of foods can be cooked on a stick. There are two methods for such cooking—end-of-the-stick cooking and kabob or whole-stick cooking.

End-of-the-Stick Cooking

When using the first method, place the food on the end of the stick and rotate so the foods cook evenly. Hot dogs and marshmallows are the most common items cooked this way. Remember, the larger the item, the farther it should be held away from the coals.

Hot dogs, apples and bread can be cooked to perfection on a stick

Kabob or Whole-Stick Cooking

The second stick cooking method creates a kabob by sliding pieces of a variety of meats, fruits and vegetables along the entire thin stick or skewer. Visually attractive and taste-tempting, kabobs can be served as a main dish, salad, or dessert—or even as all three in a single meal. A tasty and creative way to serve kabobs is to arrange a selection of many different foods on serving plates and let each person assemble his or her own kabob. Because they often include an assortment of tastes, textures and colors, kabobs are a highly popular and very versatile menu choice. Entertaining either out of doors or at home with kabobs is wonderful.

For evenly cooked, flavorful and attractive kabobs, select foods requiring about the same cooking time. If a variety of cooking times is needed, the kabob will be both overdone and underdone. If you want to use cherry tomatoes or banana chunks that require less cooking, add these toward the end of the cooking time. Also, use fairly uniform sizes for even cooking. Small food pieces may pop or split if the skewer is too large for the food.

Thread food pieces directly through the centers so the heavy side will not droop closer to the flame and possibly fall into the coals. A second skewer can be added side-by-side for more support. Place kabobs above the coals on a grill or griddle. If the fire is too hot, food that is well

Select foods to skewer that require similar cook times

cooked on the outside may be undercooked in the center. When using small bamboo skewers, remember to soak them in water beforehand so that the wood does not ignite.

Meat kabobs

Tender "even size" cuts of meat cook best. Meats require moisture and fat to tenderize, and stick cooking is a dry-heat method. To use less-tender cuts of meat, marinate for several hours in the refrigerator before you plan to cook. An acid-base marinade (such as orange or lemon juice, vinegar or tomato juice) helps to tenderize meat and add more flavor.

A second skewer can add additional stability to kabobs

Spit Cooking

Spit cooking is similar to cooking kabobs over open coals, except that it usually includes a larger-size portion of food (such as a whole chicken rather than smaller pieces of meat). From Cornish game hens to roasts and ham—even a whole pig—all are adaptable to spit cooking. A spit or rotisserie motor can be purchased commercially or improvised if you prefer not to turn the spit by hand and are planning to cook where electricity is available.

Attach meat to the spit, centering and balancing it so that it turns evenly. Secure the wings and legs of poultry firmly to the body so they do not stick out and burn. You may want to shield or cover protruding parts with foil to prevent overcooking.

Place the food evenly balanced on the spit above the cooking coals and begin turning the handle. A medium-sized food such as a chicken should cook about 8 or 10 inches from the coals. As with end-of-the-stick cooking, larger pieces should be cooked farther away and smaller pieces should be closer to the heat. Watch during cooking so that you can adjust the height of the spit if the meat is cooking too slowly or too quickly. Also, make sure that the meat continues to turn slowly for even cooking.

Methods of Spit Cooking

Bricks and dowels support and stabilize roasting food

- One method of spit cooking requires a stick about 3/4 inch in diameter and 1 to 2 feet longer than the food to be cooked. A second, smaller stick can be lashed onto this stick as a handle for easy turning. To construct the spit, cut two forked sticks tall enough so that the spit will rest two feet above the ground. You may also use a stack of flat rocks to support the spit if they are available in the area. Bricks can also be stacked to form a support for the spit. An added bonus is that you can anchor the stick through holes in the brick.

- A metal pipe can also be used as a spit. Again, it is helpful to drill holes through the middle so that foods can be secured to the pipe with wire. Select bricks that have holes in the center, stack them on opposite sides of the coals where the spit is to be supported, and suspend the spit across the middle. The cooking temperature is easily adjusted by removing or adding one or more bricks to move food closer and increase the heat. To lower heat, add additional bricks underneath the spit to raise the food higher. If you use a metal pipe, determine its length by measuring the length of food you plan to cook and add 2 feet. Drill two or more holes in the center of the pipe for threading wire to secure food tightly. A metal spit may have a handle welded on one end to make it turn more easily.

- Use sturdy forked sticks to support the spit, or prepare two metal pipes to hold the spit by welding three U-shaped pieces of half pipe to the sides of two 3-foot pieces of pipe. The two pipes will serve as brackets, making it possible to change the height of the spit. You may also substitute stacked rocks or bricks to hold the spit.

Marinating and Basting the Meat

Before you roast meat on a spit, it can be marinated to tenderize and add flavor. Add a basting sauce for additional flavor when the meat has almost finished cooking. If you use a basting sauce with a high sugar content, such as a barbecue sauce, wait until the last 15 minutes of cooking, because sugar can caramelize and cause the surface of the meat to burn.

MINI-MOZZARELLA KABOBS

2 cloves garlic, well crushed, or 2 teaspoons garlic paste

1 cup balsamic vinaigrette dressing (page 184)

2 pounds cherry tomatoes

3 pounds fresh mini-mozzarella balls, drained

3 ounces fresh basil leaves, about 40 to 50 leaves

12 to 15 skewers

Grill and At Home

In a 1-gallon plastic self-sealing bag, combine garlic, vinaigrette, tomatoes and cheese and chill in the refrigerator or cooler overnight.

Thread tomatoes and cheese balls, alternating with basil leaves, onto skewers and cook on your grill, turning often, until the cheese is slightly browned. Makes 12 to 15 kabobs.

STUFFED MUSHROOMS

18 to 20 medium mushrooms, cleaned and stemmed

1 (2.5-ounce) can deviled ham

1 (5-ounce) jar cocktail onions

10 cherry tomatoes

1/4 cup (1/2 stick) butter or margarine, melted

10 skewers

Grill and At Home

Fill mushroom caps with deviled ham. Place two caps together facing each other and thread onto skewer alternating with onions and tomatoes. Brush evenly with melted butter. Grill or barbecue over hot coals, turning often, until mushrooms are tender. Serve warm. Makes 10 kabobs.

BREAD ON A STICK

This is a wonderfully delicious recipe to share when sitting around a campfire.

- 1 dowel or roasting stick for each person
- 1 box Bisquick™ mix (number served determines the size)
- 1 cup water, in a bottle
- 1/2 cup (1 stick) butter or margarine
- 1 cup honey or jam

Grill and At Home

With the end of the stick, make a little well in the open box of Bisquick. Pour 1 tablespoon of water into the well. Place the stick in the well and begin stirring until a small ball of dough forms around the stick. Lift the stick out of the box and press the dough firmly around the end of the stick. Pass the box and water bottle to the next person to repeat.

Grill the dough stick over a bed of hot coals and turn often.

Make a well in the Bisquick™

Pour water into the well

Stir with the end of the stick to form a ball of dough

Mold the dough onto the stick to cook over the coals

When it is golden brown and cooked throughout, slide it off the stick. Butter and slather with honey or jam. Sit back and enjoy until the box makes its way again to you.

• A large box of Bisquick serves over 20.

SAUSAGE AND PINEAPPLE KABOBS

2 pounds Polish sausage or kielbasa, cut into triangles, precooked

2 (15-ounce) cans pineapple chunks, drained (reserving 1/2 cup juice)

1 pound cherry tomatoes

10 to 12 skewers

1 cup barbecue sauce

Grill and At Home

Thread precooked sausage, pineapple and tomatoes onto skewers. In a small bowl, combine barbecue sauce and juice and baste skewers. Grill over a bed of hot coals, turning and basting often. Makes 10 to 12 kabobs.

HAM SUPREME KABOBS

12 ham slices, thinly sliced

1/2 cup prepared mustard

1 (6-ounce) can whole ripe olives

1 (5-ounce) jar cocktail onions, drained

6 cherry tomatoes

6 skewers

Grill and At Home

Spread each ham slice with mustard. Fold into bite-sized pieces (mustard side in) and thread on skewers, alternating with olives, onions and tomatoes. Grill over a bed of hot coals, turning often, until ham is warmed through. Serve immediately. Serves 6.

MEAT LOAF ON A STICK

1 cup cornflakes
1 pound ground beef
1 egg
1/2 onion, chopped
1 teaspoon salt
1/8 teaspoon pepper
1/2 teaspoon prepared mustard

Foil and At Home

In a 1-gallon plastic self-sealing bag, add cornflakes and squeeze to crush. Add ground beef, egg, onion, salt, pepper and mustard and squeeze, mixing well. For each person, wrap a small quantity of this mixture around the end of a stick, making an oblong shape. Wrap foil around the meat and part of the stick and seal it using the drugstore wrap (pages 52–53). Grill over a bed of hot coals, turning often to cook evenly, about 20 to 25 minutes. Serves 3 to 4.

• Prop up the stick with a rock and turn it over from time to time.

TURKEY AND BACON KABOBS

1 pound bacon slices, cut in half
2 pounds turkey breast, fully cooked, cut into 1-inch cubes
12 to 16 kabob sticks
1 box toothpicks
2 zucchini squash, cut into chunks
1 red onion, cut into squares
1 cup lemon vinaigrette dressing (page 185)

Grill and At Home

Wrap bacon around turkey cubes, securing each with a toothpick. Thread onto skewers, alternating with turkey, squash, and onion. Baste with the dressing. Grill, turning and basting often, until squash is tender. Makes 12 to 16 kabobs.

Canned potatoes wrapped with bacon can be added to or substituted in the kabob.

TERIYAKI MEAT STICKS

A terrific recipe for an appetizer and taste-tested for many years!

1 recipe teriyaki marinade (page 183)
1 (1-gallon) plastic self-sealing bag
2 pounds sirloin steak, sliced diagonally across the grain to 1/8-inch thick
6 to 8 skewers

• Ask your butcher to slice the meat for you, or partially freeze to slice more easily.

Grill and At Home

In a 1-gallon plastic self-sealing bag add steak slices; cover with marinade and place in a cooler or refrigerator overnight. Thread meat onto skewers. Grill, turning occasionally, until meat is cooked to desired doneness. Makes 6 to 8 kabobs.

Crowd-pleasing teriyaki meat sticks

HOT DOG ON A STICK

1 stick per person
6 hot dogs
6 hot dog buns
Condiments such as mustard, ketchup, relish, etc.

Grill and At Home

Thread hot dogs onto a long stick. Grill by holding stick over hot coals, turning often until all sides are evenly browned. Place in a bun and add condiments of your choice. Serves 4 to 6.

• For a delicious variation, wrap the hot dogs in bacon and secure with toothpicks.

APPLE PIE ON A STICK

This wonderful fix-it-yourself dessert is one of my favorites!

1 cup sugar
1 tablespoon cinnamon
4 dowels or roasting sticks
4 cooking apples

In a small bowl, mix together sugar and cinnamon and set aside. Push the stick or dowel through the top of the apple to the bottom until the apple is secure. Roast the apple 2 to 3 inches above the bed of hot coals and turn frequently. (As the apple cooks, the skin starts to brown and the juice dribbles out.) When the skin is loose,

Easiest dessert ever: Apple pie on a stick cooking on a flowerpot

remove the apple from the coals but leave it on the stick. Peel the skin off the apple, being careful not to burn yourself because the apple is very hot.

Roll the apple in the mixture; then return it to roast over the coals (the sugar and cinnamon will form a glaze on the apple). Be careful not to get it so close to the fire that it burns. Remove the apple from the coals and let it cool. Slice thin pieces and eat your "apple pie on a stick." Again roll in sugar mixture, return to hot coals, slice and eat, and repeat until apple is gone. Serves 4.

• The best cooking apples are Jonathan, Rome or Granny Smith, because the skin peels off easily when heated.

Cherry-Coconut Cake

CHERRY-COCONUT CAKE
1 (8-ounce) jar cherry, apricot or strawberry jam
1 (1-pound) pound cake, cut into 1-inch cubes
1 cup shredded coconut
1 (8-ounce) jar maraschino cherries

Grill and At Home

Spread the jam on all sides of cake pieces. Roll in coconut. Thread cake bits on a skewer, alternating with maraschino cherries. Roast over a grill, barbecue or bed of hot coals until coconut is browned. Serves 6 to 8.

CHOCOLATE FONDUE KABOBS

2 cups chocolate or fudge sauce
1 (1-pound) pound cake, cut into 1-inch cubes
3 to 4 bananas, cut into thick slices
2 (10-ounce) cans mandarin oranges, drained
12 to 15 kabob sticks

Grill and At Home

In a pan of warm water, heat chocolate or fudge sauce in the bottle with the lid removed. Thread cake cubes, bananas and orange sections alternately onto the sticks. Grill or barbecue, turning 2 to 3 times as they heat. (This should only take a few minutes to warm them with a few grill marks.) Serve with warm sauce. Serves 6 to 8.

• Oil your grill before cooking so the cake cubes don't stick.

SHAGGY DOGS

1 (16-ounce) package large marshmallows
1 cup chocolate or caramel syrup, heated
1 cup shredded coconut
8 sticks

Roast each marshmallow on a stick over a bed of hot coals until golden brown. Dip into warm syrup and roll in coconut to serve. Serves 8 or more.

Shaggy Dogs are a fun and delicious alternative to S'mores

CHAPTER 3

Aluminum Foil Cooking

I've been accused of owning an aluminum foil company because I use and recommend foil so much for outdoor cooking. Foil assists with easy food storage, preparation, cooking—and even easier cleanup. One advantage of foil cooking is that each dinner guest, including small children, can assemble ingredients for their meal and then watch their own food "packet" cook to the desired doneness.

Boy Scouts in particular are experts at preparing and grilling the famous **Hobo Dinner** (page 57). My favorite is the foil-wrapped **Banana Boat** which uses marshmallows and chocolate chips and cooks in a banana peel (page 60). Recently, I overheard a small girl tug at her father, point to me, and whisper, "Daddy, that's the banana boat lady." I knew I had made an impression. You too can make memories with your loved ones by introducing them to the fun and simplicity of outdoor foil cooking.

Aluminum foil is a versatile material for cooking and wrapping food. It can be used for both hot and cold foods and is the modern version of cooking with leaves and clay. Introduced in 1947, aluminum foil has become an increasingly popular cooking material and a mainstay in every kitchen. It is 95 percent aluminum, with iron and silicon added to promote strength and puncture resistance. It can be purchased in regular, heavy-duty and extra-heavy-duty thickness. The heavier weights are often preferred for outdoor cooking because of their additional strength.

Aluminum foil can be shaped into a homemade pan using extra-heavy-duty aluminum foil. Cut a piece of foil and place it inside another pan, molding the desired shape. Fold down the excess on the sides, giving the pan extra durability. This homemade pan eliminates a dish to wash.

Drugstore Wrap

Cut one or two pieces of lightweight foil or one piece of heavy-duty or extra-heavy-duty foil twice the distance around the item to be wrapped.

- Arrange food in the center of one piece of foil.
- Bring opposite sides of the foil together and fold down in small 1/2-inch folds until package can no longer be folded.
- Flatten the two sides of the package, then roll the open edges toward the center in small folds. Edges of the package must be tightly sealed.
- If the package needs to be wrapped again for strength, place the folded top of the package upside down in the center of another piece of foil and repeat.

One advantage of foil-wrapped parcels, or "tin foil dinners," is that they can be prepared, seasoned and packed in advance of cooking. Everyone can make his or her own dinner and season it. This cuts down on preparation time and gives everyone an activity. Another plus is that these dinners will hold their heat for 10 to 15 minutes. You can enjoy dinner served directly out of the foil wrap.

Place food in the middle of 1 to 2 sheets of foil for the drugstore wrap

Fold in half-inch intervals, starting at the ends and working toward the center

Roll open ends toward the center to seal for perfect packets

BUTTERNUT SQUASH WITH APPLES

18-inch-wide aluminum foil
2 tablespoons oil
1 butternut squash, peeled and sliced into 1/2-inch
    slices
2 cooking apples, peeled and sliced
1/4 cup (1/2 stick) butter or margarine
1/4 cup brown sugar
1/2 teaspoon cinnamon
1/2 teaspoon nutmeg

Foil and At Home

Cut 4 squares of foil and brush with oil. Place 1/4 of the squash and 1/4 of the apple slices on each square. Top the mixture with 1 tablespoon butter and 1 tablespoon brown sugar. Sprinkle with cinnamon and nutmeg. Seal, using the drugstore wrap (page 52). Bake on grill or hot coals, turning occasionally, for 40 to 45 minutes, or until tender. Serve as a main dish or a side dish. Serves 6 to 8.

ONIONS AND MUSHROOMS

18-inch heavy-duty aluminum foil
2 large onions, sliced and separated into rings
1 pound portobello mushrooms, sliced
1/4 cup (1/2 stick) butter or margarine
1 teaspoon garlic powder
1/4 teaspoon salt
1/8 teaspoon pepper

Foil and At Home

Cut 4 squares of aluminum foil. Place divided onion slices onto squares; place mushroom slices on top of onions. Dot each package with 1 tablespoon butter, and sprinkle with garlic powder, salt and pepper. Seal, using the drugstore wrap (page 52). Cook on a grill over a bed of hot coals for 10 to 15 minutes on each side. Serve as an appetizer or side dish. Serves 4.

TOMATO AND CHEESE CROSTINI

A favorite recipe you'll prepare often as an appetizer, lunch or delicious side dish with meat. In Italian crostini means "little toast." Usually brushed with olive oil, it may have a topping of cheese, shrimp, paté or this combination of tomatoes and herbs.

8 slices French bread
2 tablespoons oil
1 tablespoon fresh parsley, minced
2 cloves garlic, finely mashed
3 to 4 small ripe tomatoes, thinly sliced
Salt
Pepper
8 slices fontina cheese
18-inch heavy-duty aluminum foil

Foil and At Home

Grill bread on a rack over a bed of hot coals until toasted on both sides. In a small bowl, mix oil, parsley and garlic. Brush evenly onto four bread slices. Salt and pepper, as desired. Place tomatoes on oil and herb mixture and top with cheese and remaining bread slices. Wrap in foil and heat on a grill over hot coals until cheese is slightly melted, about 5 minutes. Serve as an appetizer or sandwich. Serves 4.

IRONED CHEESE SANDWICH

Ironing is fun when you get to eat the results. Try this at home.

Iron and ironing board
Aluminum foil
1 tablespoon butter or margarine, softened
2 slices bread
1 slice Cheddar cheese

Foil and At Home

Set up iron and ironing board. Place a sheet of foil on the ironing board. Butter one side of each bread slice. Sandwich cheese between unbuttered bread sides. Wrap in foil. Iron (cotton setting) on both sides until toasty brown and cheese has melted. Serve 1 grilled sandwich with an ironed shirt!

CORN ON THE COB

Always cook corn with the husks on to protect it from burning during cooking. The corn is much sweeter than when cooked in water.

Aluminum foil
Ears of corn with husks
Butter or margarine, softened
Salt
Pepper

Foil and At Home

Method #1—Corn with husk (preferred)

Peel back the husks from the ears. Remove the silk. Spread with butter; season with salt and pepper. Pull the husks over the ears of corn and wrap individually in aluminum foil. Cook on a bed of hot coals for 10 to 15 minutes, turning frequently.

Method #2—Corn without husk

Brush ears with butter. Add salt and pepper. Wrap each ear individually in aluminum foil and cook on grill over a bed of hot coals for 15 to 20 minutes, turning frequently.

HAM AND CHEESE BAGUETTE

A *baguette* is a long, semi-hard French roll.

1/4 cup (1/2 stick) butter or margarine, softened
2 teaspoons Dijon mustard
1 baguette roll, split in half lengthwise
12 to 16 ham slices, thinly sliced
8 ounces cheese, sliced (see •)
18-inch heavy-duty aluminum foil

• For this great-tasting sandwich, you may use any cheese you prefer. I love to make it with Brie or Camembert.

Foil and Grill

In a small dish, mix butter and mustard; spread mixture on one half of the baguette. Layer with ham, cheese and the other half of the baguette. Wrap in foil. Grill 2 to 3 inches above a bed of hot coals for 10 to 15 minutes, or until cheese is completely melted. Cut into several sections to serve as an appetizer or sandwich. Serves 6.

• Excellent made with thick-sliced honey-baked ham.

HOBO DINNER

18-inch heavy-duty aluminum foil
2 carrots, peeled and thinly sliced
2 medium potatoes, peeled and thinly sliced
2 onions, sliced
1 pound ground beef, shaped into four patties
1 teaspoon salt
1/2 teaspoon pepper

Foil and At Home

Cut 4 squares of foil. Divide vegetables into 4 equal portions. Layer with one-half carrots, potatoes, onions and ground beef; finish with onions, potatoes and carrots in that order. Season with salt and pepper. Seal using the drugstore wrap (page 52). Cook on a bed of hot coals for 15 minutes on each side. Serve as a main dish or supper. Serves 4.

• Breast of chicken or fish fillets can be substituted for ground beef patties. Cooking time may need adjusting.

ROASTED TOAST

18-inch heavy-duty aluminum foil
Nonstick cooking spray
Bread

Foil and At Home

The easiest way to make toast outdoors is to place a sheet of heavy-duty aluminum foil directly onto the hot coals. Spray the foil with nonstick cooking spray. Carefully cook bread slices on the hot foil, moving often while toasting to avoid hot spots. Turn over after 1 minute and repeat. This also works well on an outdoor griddle or grill.

CHICKEN IN A POCKET

18-inch heavy-duty aluminum foil
2 tablespoons oil
4 chicken breasts or 8 thighs
4 green onions, topped
Fresh ginger, cut in 4 (quarter-size) thin slices
Fresh lemon, cut in 4 (1/4-inch thick) slices

Foil and At Home

Cut 4 squares of foil. Oil each square and place 1 chicken breast on each piece of foil; top with 1 green onion, 1 slice of ginger and 1 slice of lemon. Wrap packages using the drugstore wrap (page 52). Grill above a bed of hot coals for 20 minutes on each side. Serve as a lunch or dinner. Serves 4.

MEAT LOAF IN AN ONION

This is one of my signature recipes and is wonderful for a large group. Each person makes his or her own.

1 pound lean ground beef
1 egg
1/4 cup cracker crumbs
1/4 cup tomato sauce
1/2 teaspoon salt
1/8 teaspoon pepper
1/2 teaspoon dry mustard
4 large onions, peeled and halved (see •)
18-inch heavy-duty aluminum foil

• Cut off the root at the bottom end of the onion so that removal of the center is easy. The removed center of the onion can be diced and combined with ingredients or used later.

Foil

In a 1-gallon plastic self-sealing bag, combine ground beef, egg, cracker crumbs, tomato sauce, salt, pepper and dry mustard and mix by squeezing. Set aside.

Savory meat loaf in an onion, cooked in foil

Cut onions in half horizontally and remove center part of onion, leaving a 3/4-inch-thick shell. Divide meat mixture into 4 portions and roll into balls. Place in the center of the 4 onion halves. Put onions back together. Wrap each onion in foil using the drugstore wrap (page 52). Cook over a bed of hot coals for 15 to 20 minutes per side. Serve as a lunch or dinner. Serves 4.

At Home

Cook at 350°F. in the oven for 45 to 50 minutes, or until the ground beef and onion are cooked.

BANANA BOAT

18-inch heavy-duty aluminum foil
1 banana, unpeeled
Miniature marshmallows
Milk chocolate chips or broken candy bars

Foil and At Home

Cut a slit lengthwise about two-thirds of the way through the banana from the stem to the base. Fill the slit with miniature marshmallows and milk chocolate chips or broken pieces of chocolate bars. (I like to use milk chocolate chips because they melt in your mouth, in your hand—they melt everywhere.) To heat the banana boat, wrap in foil and cook on hot coals for five minutes, or until the chocolate and marshmallows have melted. Serve as a snack, a dessert or a treat around the campfire.

• If you leave the boats in the coals too long, the bananas will liquefy.

• You can also create a fruit "banana boat" by using maraschino cherries, shredded coconut, nuts and pineapple.

One of my favorites, the banana boat

CHAPTER 4

Dutch Oven Cooking

T he Dutch oven is the most versatile utensil for outdoor cooking. No other piece of equipment brings
the outdoors into my everyday city life like the Dutch
oven. It works as a combination oven/range, and can be used
for meats or main courses, side dishes, breads, and—best of
all—desserts.

I share my outdoor life with friends and family by delivering
a steaming, delicious **Pineapple Upside-Down "birthday"
Cake** (page 210). Requests for my **Pistol Rock Chicken** and
Enchilada Pie (pages 145 and 149) are numerous. As one of
the World Dutch Oven Cooking Contest judges for several
years, I have tasted succulent shrimp, standing rib roasts,
mouth-watering breads and even perfect pies baked inside
Dutch ovens. There's virtually no limit to the uses for the creative outdoor cook. I have included purchasing information,
seasoning and reseasoning instructions, temperature adjustments, safety instructions and some of my all-time favorite
recipes for you and your guests to enjoy elegant and easy
Dutch oven foods.

Dutch ovens, one of the oldest cooking implements, are cast-iron pots of varying sizes, from 5 to 16 inches in diameter. They hold heat well for long periods of time. Dutch ovens have been a staple of American cooking since the early history of the United States. They continue to be used today as an easy way to cook delicious meals. An added bonus is that their use increases the iron nutrient in your diet.

Modern Dutch ovens began as black ironware, which was used throughout Europe for many years. England was a primary exporter of cast-iron pots, skillets and kettles through its worldwide fleet. In early America, Dutch traders traveled from door to door selling household goods such as the baking ovens. Legend dictates they were named "Dutch ovens" after the nationality of the peddlers who sold them.

Family journals from early America tell of many people who relied on their cast-iron kettles and Dutch ovens for everyday cooking. Paul Revere is often credited with developing the flat-topped, three-legged Dutch oven.

A Dutch oven is the most versatile pot for outdoor cooking. It uses either dry or moist heat in a variety of cooking techniques such as baking, stewing, braising and frying.

Outdoor and Indoor Dutch Ovens

Outdoor Dutch Ovens

The outdoor Dutch oven has three legs and a flat lid. It is designed so that hot coals can be placed underneath and on top. A heavy metal handle is attached at two sides and curves over the top of the pot so that it is easy to hang or to carry. The lid is flat with a raised rim so that coals or briquettes can be placed on top to add additional heat for baking.

The outdoor Dutch oven can be adapted for indoor use by setting it on a cookie sheet or on its lid and then placing it into the oven. The outdoor Dutch oven can be suspended over coals, placed on the ground over coals or buried underground in coals.

The versatile Dutch oven can be used indoors or outdoors

Today, cast-iron Dutch ovens are used by hunters, campers, river runners, Scouts and family groups for outdoor cooking in the mountains, in the woods, at the beach, on patios, and in backyards.

Outdoor Dutch ovens are carried by hardware stores, outdoor recreational stores, and other general retailers and can be ordered from mail-order vendors or www.lodgemfg.com on the Web.

Indoor Dutch Ovens

The indoor Dutch oven is flat bottomed, has a dome-shaped lid and can be purchased at department and cooking stores. It is designed for use indoors in a home oven, on a range or outside on a camp stove. The indoor Dutch oven can be adapted for outdoor use by elevating it above hot coals with three rocks or bricks so hot coals can be set underneath.

To adapt the lid of an indoor Dutch oven to hold coals, create a foil ring slightly smaller in circumference than the lid of the oven. Place the foil ring onto the lid and arrange the coals inside the ring. The lid of the indoor Dutch oven also can be turned upside down to hold hot coals on top.

Purchasing a Dutch Oven

Select your Dutch oven according to when, where, and how often you will use it, and the kinds of foods you'll want to prepare in it. The more you plan to use your Dutch oven (and you'll want to use it often after you taste the mouth-watering dishes), the more you'll want to invest in a quality Dutch oven. If you plan on doing most of your cooking outside, purchase one with legs. If you plan on cooking a variety of recipes at once, buy several with legs for easy stacking. Whatever material, size or design you choose, it's always a good idea to experiment with several borrowed from family and friends before you make your final purchase.

Seasoning and Re-seasoning a Dutch Oven

Before use, your Dutch oven will require "seasoning." Wash the pot and lid in hot, soapy water to dissolve the manufacturer's protective wax residue. Wipe both the oven and lid dry with paper towels.

Because cast iron is a porous metal, you need to "season" it with vegetable oil or melted shortening before use. Pour 1 to 2 tablespoons of shortening or oil into the interior and rub with a clean cloth over the entire surface, adding more oil as necessary. Repeat the procedure, wiping an oil-dipped cloth around the sides, bottom, and lid. Be sure to absorb any extra oil so that no pools of oil remain. A nonstick cooking surface will build up as you continue to give your Dutch oven an oil treatment after every use.

The next seasoning step is to preheat a conventional oven to 350°F. Put the Dutch oven upside down on a cookie sheet placed on an oven rack. (The cookie sheet is necessary so that oil will not drip from the upside-down Dutch oven onto the heating elements of the conventional oven.) Place the lid atop the legs of the upside-down pot.

After one hour of "seasoning," turn off the heat on the conventional oven and leave the Dutch oven inside until it cools completely. (Never use water to speed the cooling; it can cause the oven to pit or warp.) After cooling, it is ready for cooking.

Cleaning and Storage

Keeping your Dutch oven clean is essential to enjoying your outdoor cooking experience. When cooking outside, use a rubber spatula to scrape out any food that remains after the meal is over. If the food is hardened and baked onto the surface, fill the bottom with water and boil and/or allow the Dutch oven to soak briefly until the food loosens and will rinse off. A mixture of salt or kosher salt and oil helps to clean without scratching your Dutch oven. Then wipe the oven clean. Dry the oven and apply a thin coat of oil to the entire surface with a paper towel.

When cooking indoors, use warm, soapy water and a non-abrasive scrubbing pad or salt to clean inside the pot. Then wipe the pot surface dry with a clean cloth or paper towel. Finally, use a paper towel or a clean cloth and cover the entire interior and exterior surface with a thin coating of oil.

It's important to the flavor of future meals and to the life of your oven that it be stored properly. Since moisture is your oven's greatest enemy, it is critical that it be stored in such a way that no moisture is allowed to remain inside. After each use, thoroughly clean, wipe dry and cover with a thin coat of oil so it is ready for the next meal. Loosely wad a handful of paper towels and place inside the pot. The towels will absorb any moisture remaining inside and create a space between the lid and the bottom to allow moisture to evaporate. Or you can roll aluminum foil to make a "snake" and arrange it as a collar on the rim of the pot, creating a space between the pot and the lid to allow moisture to evaporate.

Foil collars allow air to circulate during storing

When storing your Dutch oven for a long period of time, you may find that the oil takes on a "gummy" texture. If this occurs, heat the Dutch oven upside down on a cookie sheet at 350°F. in your oven or over glowing briquettes until the residue melts and wipe it clean with a paper towel. You might find a Dutch oven at a yard or garage sale that is so dirty or gummy that it cannot be cleaned by hand; place it in a self-cleaning conventional oven and clean it as you would clean your oven, and all of the dirt and oil will burn off. You will need to re-season your oven when you clean it this way. With proper care, you will get years of scrumptious meals, and it will be waiting for your next indoor or outdoor adventure.

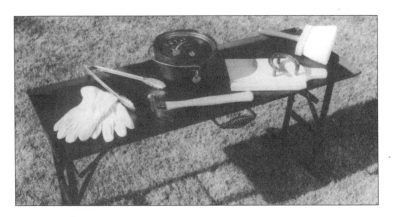

A few key accessories make Dutch oven cooking a breeze

Accessories

A wide array of accessories will be helpful—in some cases essential—to Dutch oven cooking. We suggest the following; you will find others as you refine and personalize your cooking technique.

- **Lid lifter**—allows you to remove the lid without burning your hands; the claw end of a hammer or pliers can also be used.
- **Lid holder or rack**—a rack to rest the lid on so it stays clean while you are checking the food. It can also hold an upside-down lid during cooking.
- **Leather gloves, hot pads, oven mitts or cooking shirt** (page 29)—allows you to work more freely around the Dutch oven without burning your hands.
- **Tongs**—to arrange the hot or cold briquettes.

- **Whisk broom**—to brush the briquette ashes off the lid.
- **Cutting board**—always a useful tool for a clean place to slice food.
- **Shovel**—to place hot coals on the lid.
- **Dutch oven cooking table**—a metal, fireproof table on which to cook.
- **Nylon storage bags**—lightweight storage for your Dutch oven accessories.

It is essential to have a good flat surface on which to cook. The best surface can hold heat, such as a stepping stone or heavy metal, and helps the Dutch oven retain heat during and after cooking.

Dutch Oven Cooking Basics

Virtually any method of cooking you encounter on a daily basis can be adapted for Dutch oven use—baking, braising, boiling, frying, stewing and roasting.

Temperature Control

Most baking recipes require a temperature setting of 325°F. An easy equation to get **a temperature of 325°F. within your Dutch oven** is to subtract or add the number 3 to the size of your Dutch oven to determine the number of charcoal briquettes to use underneath and on top. Find the size of the Dutch oven you use (see chart below) to know the correct number of briquettes.

DUTCH OVEN 325° TEMPERATURE BRIQUETTE QUANTITIES		
Size of Oven	*Top*	*Bottom*
8-inch	11	5
10-inch	13	7
12-inch	15	9
14-inch	17	11
16-inch	19	13

The following example uses the formula for a 12-inch Dutch oven.

- Subtract 3 from 12 which equals 9—the number of briquettes to place beneath the oven.
- Take the number 12 and add 3 which equals 15—the number of briquettes to place on the lid of the oven.

With this formula, 9 briquettes go underneath and 15 briquettes are placed on the top of the lid of a 12-inch Dutch oven to cook at 325°F. One-third of the heat will be underneath the Dutch oven, and two-thirds of the heat will be on top. Heat rises so you do not need as many coals on the bottom of the oven. Arrange briquettes so they are evenly spaced under the Dutch oven and on its lid. Also, you always need to rotate your Dutch oven a quarter turn every 15 minutes to avoid hot spots. Replace briquettes with new coals as they "burn out."

Temperature control is determined by charcoal briquette placement

Baking in a Dutch Oven

Most people would never dream of baking outdoors, but the most flavorful treats can be baked in a Dutch oven. Cake, pie, and biscuits cooked in your kitchen take about the same time in a Dutch oven. Baking can be done directly in the Dutch oven bottom, or by placing a pan in the oven elevated on rocks, canning jar rings, a Dutch oven rack, a round cookie cooling rack or small wads of foil. When elevating your food

Rocks elevate baking pans for pies, cakes or bread

Perfect pie, baked inside a Dutch oven

in a Dutch oven, you create an oven like the one at home which allows hot air to circulate around the pan. This is the easiest way to bake in a Dutch oven.

I suggest taking a **prepared pie** with you and cooking it at your camping site. In a 12-inch Dutch oven, place 12 hot coals on the bottom and 17 on top of the lid to create a 375°F. oven and bake 30 to 40 minutes.

Roasting Foods in a Dutch Oven

Most **roasting recipes require a temperature of 375°F. or higher.** To achieve a high-temperature oven, you need to use additional coals on the lid and underneath. Preheat the Dutch oven for 10 or more minutes before filling it. For example, to reach 375°F. in a 12-inch Dutch oven, use 11 coals under the Dutch oven and 17 hot coals on the lid.

Frying Foods in a Dutch Oven

To **sauté food in a Dutch oven,** place charcoal briquettes under the oven in a checkerboard pattern, using the same number of briquettes as the size of the Dutch oven. For example, a 12-inch Dutch oven requires 12 briquettes underneath.

To **fry foods in deep oil in a Dutch oven,** place charcoal briquettes under the Dutch oven using 3 or 4 more briquettes than the size of the Dutch oven. For example, a 12-inch Dutch oven would require 15 to 16 briquettes underneath.

Simmering Foods in a Dutch Oven

For **simmering foods, start with a 325°F. oven** and let the coals cool as your food cooks. Do not replace briquettes as you would to continue baking at 325°F. Hot coals are enough to simmer foods for 1 to 1 1/2 hours, especially when you tap the ashes off which adds more oxygen to the coals.

Stacking Multiple Dutch Ovens

When cooking several different dishes at the same time, stack the pots to save space and briquettes. Stacking works best if you put the food to be *baked* at the bottom of the stack and add Dutch ovens with shorter cooking times on top. Food to be sautéed is in the smallest oven at the top of the stack. Always stack the largest Dutch oven at the bottom and decrease in size as you stack. Add three briquettes to the number of inches of each pot and put that many briquettes on each lid.

Many wonderful recipes for Dutch oven cooking are found throughout this book.

Stacked Dutch ovens for efficient and convenient cooking

CHAPTER 5

Grilling

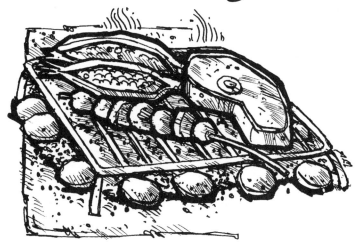

C ertainly the most popular form of outdoor cooking is
barbecuing. Whether you make a barbecue of bricks
and briquettes or buy a deluxe gas grill, you are probably one of millions who appreciates this artful cooking
method. Grilling meats, fish and poultry may be familiar, but
have you tried vegetables, fruits, or desserts on a grill? For
example, warm, juicy **Grilled Pineapple** is a treat for everyone. Peel and core each fresh pineapple; slice 1/2-inch thick.
Grill over hot coals until lightly browned on each side.
Serve warm.

There are ways to prepare an entire meal on a grill while the
dinner guests gather around and help with the basting, turning
and timing. Men, in particular, have proven to be great grill
chefs. Beyond the basics, I have discovered ways to prepare
Fried Chicken Fingers, Marinated Ahi Tuna and **Barbecued Pork Spareribs** (pages 76, 81 and 82). Hopefully, these
recipes and tips will inspire you to experiment with new ideas
and a variety of foods to get the most use and enjoyment from
your outdoor barbecue grill.

The idea of cooking outside on a grill brings back many memories of relaxed, outdoor recreation accompanied by delicious foods and wonderful friends. From sizzling steaks and hamburgers, to a quick side dish or salmon with a zesty vinaigrette dressing, grill cooking is versatile, convenient and fun. It is quickly becoming today's most popular outdoor cooking method. And we love the easy cleanup! Entertaining is much more relaxing and casual out of doors.

Many types of grills are available for outdoor cooking (see chapter 1). The key to successful grilling is effectively regulating the heat. Cooking times vary depending on the size, shape and cut of the food, and the temperature of the coals. For information on testing the temperature of the coals, see chart below.

To **test the amount of heat in a charcoal fire,** hold your palm at the cooking level. If you can keep it there:

2 seconds	=	high heat
3 seconds	=	medium-high heat
4 seconds	=	medium heat
5 seconds	=	medium-low heat
6 and over	=	low heat

Adjust heat by changing the placement of your grilling rack, if possible, or spreading out your coals using tongs to move a few to the outer rim.

Usually, food is placed at an average height of three to four inches above the coals. If you plan to grill a thick cut of meat which needs to cook longer, move it farther away from the coals so that it will cook more slowly and thoroughly. Heat cooks thinner cuts more quickly, so they

Use a meat thermometer to check your meat before serving

SAFE COOKING TEMPERATURES

Beef and Lamb
Rare . . . . 140°
Medium . . . . 160°
Well Done . . . . 170°

Chicken . . . . 175°–180°

Fish . . . . 120°–145°

Ground Meats
Beef, Lamb, Pork . . . . 160°
Chicken and Turkey . . . . 165°

Pork
Chops, Roast . . . . 150°-165°
Cured . . . . 140°

Sausage . . . . 160°

Turkey
Bone-in . . . . 180°
Boneless Roast . . . . 170°

can be placed closer to the coals. Don't crowd foods. Arrange food so that air can circulate evenly around each item.

Hibachis and kettle grills are equipped with air vents at the bottom to regulate the amount of oxygen. Opening the vents increases the heat, while closing them shuts off the oxygen flow and lowers the heat. If you are cooking on a grill with a lid, leaving the lid down allows heat to circulate and evenly cook the food without flare-ups. Lifting the lid more than is necessary in recipe instructions increases the cooking time. A squirt gun, turkey baster or spray bottle helps to eliminate flare-ups. To help determine when your food is completely cooked, use a thermometer to measure the internal temperature. This insures the meat is cooked just right.

Long-handled tools, barbecue gloves and a "cooking shirt"

(page 29) protect your hands from the heat. Use tongs or turners rather than forks that can pierce the food, causing flavorful juices to escape. To make cleanup easier, coat the grill with oil or a nonstick vegetable spray before cooking. Always trim excess fats from meat or select lean cuts to avoid flare-ups.

Carefully review recipes the first time they are prepared. This will help you to judge how the food should be grilled and how it will taste. Then feel free to utilize your creativity to customize and substitute with your favorites.

When you use a basting sauce, preheating it avoids slowing down the cooking. It is best to baste during the last 15 minutes so that the sauce won't burn. This happens more often because sugar caramelizes more quickly. The sauce can also cause the food to burn.

There are numerous recipes throughout this book in addition to the ones found in this chapter that use the grill.

Ready-to-Eat and Prepared Foods

Grilled foods are fast and convenient and also very satisfying. There is nothing better than a tender cut of meat grilled to perfection. However, there are shortcuts at the supermarket. Fully cooked meats can be put on a grill for a few minutes just to heat to serving temperature. Many come with their own sauces, which makes them even more convenient. A great variety of barbecued ribs, beef or pork, chicken breasts, whole chickens, pork tenderloins, etc., are ready for grill heating.

About Mixed Grill—

A combination of bacon, chicken, kielbasa or sausage, lamb chops, pork, steak and a tenderloin or two basted with barbecue sauce and served together is called "mixed grill." The mixed grill is frequently served with grilled vegetables. This is a nice menu choice because everyone gets to sample several different items.

Rule for Cooking Fish—

Fish cooks at a lower temperature than meats or poultry. A good rule for cooking fish is to measure the thickest part with a ruler and cook 8 to 10 minutes per inch of thickness. Fish can be baked, broiled, fried, grilled and steamed. To test fish for doneness, flake it with a fork at its thickest point. It should be opaque and the juices milky white. Overcooked fish is dry and falls apart easily. Another test is to insert a cooking thermometer at the thickest point. It should register 145°F. when fish is fully cooked.

GRILLED FISH

2 tablespoons olive oil
2 large (1/2- to 1-inch thick) fish fillets
1/2 teaspoon salt
1/8 teaspoon pepper

Camp Stove and At Home

In a large skillet, heat oil; add fish and season with salt and pepper. Cook for 2 1/2 to 4 1/2 minutes on each side, or until fish flakes and is opaque. Serves 2.

Grill

Heat grill and brush with oil. When hot, add fish fillets and cook 2 1/2 to 4 1/2 minutes per side. To prevent overcooked fish from flaking and falling into the coals, place a strip of pierced, oiled foil on the hot grill and lay fish on the foil. Be careful not to overcook. When fish flakes easily, it is fully cooked. Serves 2.

Dutch Oven Lid

Place the lid of a 12-inch Dutch oven upside down on a lid holder over 12 to 15 hot coals. Preheat the lid 5 minutes. Brush oil on hot lid, add fish and season with salt and pepper. Cook for 2 1/2 to 4 1/2 minutes on each side, or until fillets are evenly browned and flake easily. Serves 2.

FRIED CHICKEN FINGERS

1 cup all-purpose flour
1 teaspoon salt
1/2 teaspoon pepper
1 tablespoon garlic powder, optional
4 to 5 chicken breasts, skinned, boned and cut into
    strips (called "chicken tenders")
2 eggs, beaten
1 cup bread crumbs
2 tablespoons vegetable oil

In a paper sack or 1-gallon plastic self-sealing bag, add flour, salt, pepper and garlic powder. Dredge chicken in seasoned flour, shaking off excess. Dip chicken pieces in beaten eggs, one at a time, then coat with bread crumbs. Shake off excess.

Camp Stove and At Home

In a large skillet, heat oil. Brown chicken in hot oil, allowing 1/4 inch between each piece, until golden brown on each side. You may have to cook in 2 or 3 batches. Serves 4 to 6.

Grill

Heat the grill and brush with oil. When hot, place chicken fingers on grill and cook 5 to 8 minutes, until golden brown on each side. If pieces are too small and grill slots too wide, place a strip of pierced, oiled foil on the hot grill and lay chicken on the foil to cook (see tip below). Serves 4 to 6.

Dutch Oven

Heat a 12-inch Dutch oven over 12 to 15 hot coals. Add oil and brown chicken in hot oil, allowing 1/4 inch between each piece, until golden brown on each side. You may have to cook in 2 or 3 batches. Serves 4 to 6.

• Chicken tenders may be available in the meat case. They may be threaded on a skewer for easy cooking or grilling.

Rule for Cooking Pork—

Pork is leaner and higher in protein than it was 10 years ago. Trichinosis is also rarely known. Precautions should include washing anything that comes in contact with raw pork. Never taste uncooked pork. An internal temperature of 137°F. in pork will kill any Trichinoane. An increased safety margin for thermometer inaccuracy would be an internal temperature from 150° to 165°F. The 170° to 185°F. recommended in many cookbooks produces overcooked meat.

GRILLED MARINATED PORK CHOPS

2 lemons, juiced
3 tablespoons oil, divided
6 thick pork chops
1/2 cup dry rub for beef or pork (page 180)

In a small bowl, blend lemon juice and 1 tablespoon olive oil. Coat chops with the mixture, then rub the dry rub on both sides of chops. Place in 1-gallon plastic self-sealing bag and marinate overnight in refrigerator or cooler.

Camp Stove and At Home

In a large frying pan, heat 2 tablespoons oil; add chops and cook 10 to 15 minutes on each side, until meat is browned and thermometer reads 160°F. in the center. Serves 6.

Grill

Heat grill and brush with oil. When hot, place chops on grill and cook 10 to 15 minutes on each side, until meat is browned and thermometer reads 160°F. in the center. Serves 6.

Dutch Oven Lid

Place the lid of a 12-inch Dutch oven upside down on a lid holder over 12 to 15 hot coals and heat oil. Add chops and cook 10 to 15 minutes on each side, until meat is browned and thermometer reads 160°F. in the center. Serves 6.

GRILLED VEGETABLES

1/4 cup garlic and herb butter or margarine, melted
  (page 177)
1 zucchini, cut in lengthwise slices
1 yellow squash, cut in lengthwise slices
3 large white or red onions, sliced 1/2 inch thick
2 blanched artichokes, remove chokes (the furry, inedible center), and cut into 4 sections
8 large mushroom caps, halved
1/2 teaspoon salt
1/4 teaspoon pepper

• If your grill has wide spaces between the "ribs," cut vegetables big enough to prevent their falling into the fire, or grill on a piece of pierced oiled foil over hot coals.

• Most fresh *vegetables in season* are good for grilling. Brush with olive oil, turning over halfway through cooking.

Grill and At Home

Brush vegetables with garlic butter or margarine and place on the hot grill. Grill on each side for 5 to 10 minutes to brown and soften. Add salt and pepper and serve. Serves 4.

Dutch Oven Lid

Place the lid of a 12-inch Dutch oven upside down on a lid holder over 12 to 15 hot coals. When very hot, in about 10 minutes, brush vegetables with garlic butter or margarine and arrange on lid. Cook for 10 minutes on each side until browned and soft. Add salt and pepper and serve. Serves 4.

About Blanching Vegetables and Fruits—

To **blanch vegetables and fruits,** plunge into boiling water briefly and then into ice water to stop the cooking. Fruits needing blanching are peaches, pears, apricots and tomatoes. I usually blanch any vegetable that I plan to can or freeze. Blanching firms the flesh, loosens the skin and increases and sets the color and flavor.

GRILLED STEAKS

4 steaks, as desired
1/2 teaspoon salt
1/4 teaspoon pepper
2 tablespoons butter or margarine
4 tablespoons herbed butter (page 177)

Camp Stove and At Home

Season steaks with salt and pepper. In a large frying pan, heat butter. When hot, add steaks. Do not touch or move steaks until they are well seared and detach easily from the pan. Turn over and repeat, cooking to desired doneness. Serve topped with 1 tablespoon of herbed butter per steak. Serves 4.

Grill

Season steaks with salt and pepper. Heat grill very hot. Brush a little butter on both sides of the steaks and place steaks on the grill. Do not touch steaks until well seared and they detach easily from the grill (about 5 minutes). Turn over and repeat, cooking to desired doneness. Serve topped with 1 tablespoon of herbed butter per steak. Serves 4.

Dutch Oven Lid

Place the lid of a 12-inch Dutch oven upside down on a lid holder over 12 hot coals. Season steaks with salt and pepper. When lid is hot, melt the butter and add steaks to the lid. Do not touch steaks until well seared and they detach easily from the lid (about 5 minutes). Turn over and repeat, cooking to desired doneness. Serve topped with 1 tablespoon of herbed butter per steak. Serves 4.

• Tender cuts of meat such as T-bone, ribeye, Porterhouse, New York strip, pork tenderloin, filet mignon, etc., are superb for cooking outdoors.

HAMBURGERS

One pound of ground beef makes 4 servings the size of the palm of your hand. Place ground beef patties on a hot grill and cook on both sides to desired doneness. Season to taste. The following is a basic hamburger mix:

1 pound ground beef, chicken, meatless (soy), pork or turkey, or a combination
1 egg
1/2 teaspoon salt
Dash pepper
1/2 medium onion, chopped
Spices as desired
Bread or cracker crumbs
Milk to moisten

Grill and At Home

In a 1-gallon plastic self-sealing bag, combine meat, egg, salt, pepper, onion, spices, bread or cracker crumbs and milk. Push air out of the bag and seal. Squeeze to mix thoroughly. Shape into 4 patties. Grill over hot coals, turning over after 5 minutes, to desired doneness. Serve with your choice of toppings below. Serves 4.

Fun Toppings:

- Chili peppers with Monterey Jack cheese
- Grilled onions with spinach and bacon
- Lettuce, tomatoes, onions and avocado slices
- Onions and/or green peppers, chopped
- Pepperoni, sliced
- Shredded cheese of your choice
- Tomato slices with mozzarella cheese
- Tomatoes, garlic paste and fresh basil

Saucy Sauces:

- Barbecue sauce
- Chili
- Cocktail sauce
- Herbed butter
- Marinara sauce
- Nacho cheese sauce

MARINATED CHINESE STEAK
2 pounds sirloin steak, London broil or flank steak
1 recipe Oriental marinade for beef (page 182)

Grill and At Home

Pierce steak with a fork or sharp knife. In a 1-gallon plastic self-sealing bag, add steak and pour marinade into the bag. Seal and marinate in the refrigerator or cooler for at least 4 hours and preferably overnight.

Remove steaks from the bag, pat dry with a paper towel and place on heated grill. Cook 3 to 4 minutes per side, depending on desired doneness. Slice steak thinly across the grain and serve. Serves 4 to 6.

MARINATED AHI TUNA
1 recipe teriyaki marinade (page 183)
1 lemon
Vegetable oil
4 (6- to -8-ounce) Ahi tuna steaks

Grill and At Home

In a 1-gallon plastic self-sealing bag, add teriyaki marinade and juice of 1 lemon. Add tuna steaks; seal and store in a refrigerator or cooler for at least 1 hour. On a hot grill, add fish and cook 2 1/2 to 4 minutes per side. In a saucepan, boil leftover marinade and serve with the fish. Serves 4.

Dutch Oven Lid

In a 1-gallon plastic self-sealing bag, add teriyaki marinade and juice of 1 lemon. Add tuna steaks; seal and store in a refrigerator or cooler for at least 1 hour.

Place the lid of a 12-inch Dutch oven upside-down on a small rack or lid holder over 12 hot coals and heat until very hot. Brush with a little oil and add tuna. Cook 2 1/2 to 4 minutes per side. In a saucepan boil leftover marinade and serve with the fish. Serves 4.

• Leftover marinade must always be boiled before serving with cooked food to avoid cross contamination.

BARBECUED PORK SPARERIBS

Rebecca's super sparerib supper from a super cook.

4 country-style ribs
1 cup barbecue sauce (page 179)

Grill and At Home

In a large saucepan, cover ribs with water and boil 45 to 60 minutes until tender. Pour off water and add barbecue sauce. Grill over hot coals 10 minutes on each side until brown and crispy and evenly cooked. Brush with barbecue sauce the last 5 minutes on each side. Serve with the extra sauce. Serves 4.

About Spareribs—

Two forms of spareribs are common—*country-style* (meaty) spareribs or a *rack* of ribs without the extra meat. They are quite fatty which gives a better flavor. You might prefer to boil or pressure cook the ribs before grilling to tenderize and remove some of the fat. Marinating is a popular way to gain flavor. Add barbecue sauce near the end to prevent burning.

Kabob Bar

Kabobs are called *brochette* meaning skewer in French; *shish kebabs* meaning chunks of marinated meat, fish or vegetables threaded on a skewer in the Middle East; and *saté* meaning spicy meat, poultry or seafood threaded onto skewers and often served with a spicy peanut sauce in Indonesia.

Metal skewers with a flat blade will keep food from turning during cooking. Bamboo sticks can be used but need soaking before cooking. Twist meat strips or alternate with vegetables when threading onto skewers or sticks. A wonderful way to entertain a small or large crowd is to prepare a selection of meat or fish, vegetables or fruits and even dessert foods so each person can make his or her own kabobs. Be careful to combine sizes, shapes and foods that cook in about the same amount of time. A variety of basting sauces should also be provided. Grill kabobs over hot coals until evenly cooked and baste near the end of the cooking time. For ideas, see pages 37–49.

CHAPTER 6

Novelty Cooking

D uring thousands of television appearances, seen by millions of viewers, I found the most enthusiastic response was to my innovative "novelty" cooking ideas. An element of fun is always included with all my outdoor recipes and camping trips. Many creative ideas have endured to become "classics" and, hopefully, will be enjoyed by future generations too.

Johnny Carson helped me cook bacon and eggs in a paper sack; Tom Brokaw prepared ice cream in a tin can; Jane Pauley boiled water in a paper cup and Martin Short, on the premiere episode of his TV show, carried around a whole chicken as it cooked in his backpack. I invite you to share these inventive, delightful ideas with your family and friends, and you'll collect as many memorable experiences as I have. They may become your classics.

Two of the most enjoyable and creative results of cooking outdoors are the innovation and experimentation involved. In outdoor cooking, it's fun to explore both a variety of cooking methods and a variety of utensils. It's also interesting and fun to cook with items that weren't originally designed as utensils but can be improvised as cooking equipment. The possibilities for novelty cooking are limited only by your imagination. Try some of the following ideas; exercise your imagination and create your own new ideas for "novelty" cooking.

BACKPACK CHICKEN

Cook your chicken in a backpack while going on a hike.

1 (3-pound) whole chicken
18-inch heavy-duty aluminum foil
3 rocks (see first • below)
Tongs
Heavy gloves
2-inch stack of newspaper
1 cup barbecue sauce
1 medium-size backpack

The key to "backpack cooking" a chicken is in selecting the right kinds and sizes of rocks that will be heated to cook the chicken. Select rocks that are completely dry and have not been sitting in water or in a stream bed. **When wet rocks are heated, they can pop open and even explode.** Also, avoid using sandstone or limestone rock as they are too porous.

• Select one rock that is the size of both your hands clasped together. This should fill the cavity of the chicken. Select two rocks the size of a loose open fist, for placing under the wings during cooking. Scrub the rocks with soap and water and thoroughly dry. (Don't worry—the small amount of time the rocks are wet while being washed will not cause them to explode.)
• If you are concerned about the cleanliness of the rocks, wrap them in foil.
• Build a campfire.
• Always wear heavy gloves when working with hot rocks. After cleaning the rocks, set them on the open fire and allow

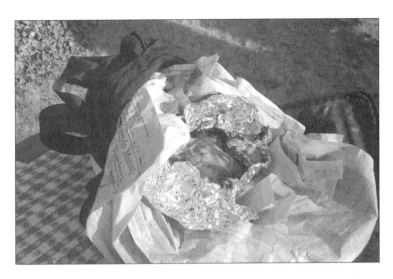

Unpack your backpack and enjoy delectable barbecue-sauced chicken!

to heat for 35 to 45 minutes. With tongs or a stick turn over the rocks and leave in the fire until they are thoroughly heated. Rocks can be heated on a very hot bed of charcoal briquettes or over gas burners; turn the rocks frequently to heat through evenly.

• While the rocks are heating, locate your two-inch pile of newspapers. Take each section of newspaper and open it as if you were reading the center pages. Stack the newspapers on top of each other until you have a one-inch stack.

• Clean the chicken and place it in the center of a sheet of 18-inch heavy-duty aluminum foil large enough to go around the chicken with about 7 inches left on each side.

• Put on heavy gloves. Stretch the chicken cavity and insert the largest hot rock. Place another rock under each wing.

• Check the rocks to see that they are sizzling and the chicken is beginning to cook. Heat from the rocks actually cooks the chicken. Pour 1 cup of barbecue sauce over the chicken.

• Using the drugstore wrap (page 52), bring the foil sides together at the top of the chicken, roll into small folds, flatten the sides and roll ends to the center. Place the wrapped chicken at the corner of the newspaper pile. Roll the chicken again and again in the newspapers, tucking in the sides as you roll. Use all of the newspapers around the chicken. Place the wrapped package inside the backpack. If it feels too warm against your back, add more layers of newspaper between the wrapped chicken and the backpack. Papers are insulation to hold the heat inside the chicken. The internal temperature of the chicken should reach 175°F. Two to three hours later, unwrap and enjoy!

CAR MANIFOLD COOKING

Cooking on the manifold is really amazing. You can be driving to your destination while your food is actually cooking under the hood. This inventive way of cooking is possible if you can find an open area on your car's manifold—a consistently hot part of the engine.

To find the manifold, look under the car and locate the exhaust. Follow it into the engine . . . the point where the pipes connect into the engine is the manifold. If there is an open area on the manifold where you can secure a foil package with wire, if needed, you can cook while you travel.

Place the food on a piece of heavy-duty foil and wrap it using the drugstore wrap (page 52). Seal it tightly to protect against juice leakage. Once you've secured the foil package to the manifold, begin driving. The food will cook about as fast as it would at medium temperature in a home range. The first time you will have to watch it carefully because the heat output

Using the heat of your car's engine to cook is easy!

differs from car to car. When the food is about half cooked, stop and turn it over. My car takes about 10 miles per side to cook a hamburger patty. Imagine stopping on the side of the road to turn your hamburger and a police officer pulls over to see if he can help. Just tell him you are turning your hamburger. This will be a great story for him to add to his repertoire.

This method can add a note of whimsy to any long-distance trip. If your manifold is big enough and you are planning to drive from three to four hours, you could cook a chicken. Meat loaf is another manifold favorite. SUVs tend to have excellent manifolds for this type of novelty cooking.

To attract further attention, you can do the washing in the trunk as your hamburger cooks on the manifold. Imagine this scenario! When traveling or just running afternoon errands, take along a large plastic container with a tight-fitting lid. Fill the container half full with hot water and add your laundry, including a few pairs of socks and detergent. Cover the container and anchor it in your trunk so it will not tip over. As you are driving, the clothes will be agitating. In my town there are so many ruts and potholes that I get heavy-duty agitation. If you need dry socks for your child's soccer match, just stop at a 7-11 and rinse them in the wash room. Now roll down your car window and drape the tops of the socks over the edge, leaving the majority hanging outside the window. Roll up the window and off you go. Now you are set. Dinner is cooking on the manifold, the washing is in the trunk, and the socks are drying out the window. What more could you ask for an afternoon of fun!

Your clothes dryer was never this much fun

HAMBURGERS ON A SHOVEL

The shovel makes a great long-handled frying pan.

Aluminum foil
Flat-nosed shovel, cleaned
Ground beef, as needed
Hamburger buns, as needed

Spread aluminum foil tightly around the shovel. Arrange the ground beef patties on the shovel. Cook over hot coals to the desired doneness. The drippings will flow off the shovel. Serve on a bun with your favorite condiments.

Cooking hamburgers on a shovel

Cooking hot dogs on a pitchfork

PITCHFORK HOT DOGS

One cooker cooks 5 dogs!

Hot dogs, as needed
Pitchfork
Hot dog buns, as needed

Place hot dogs on each pitchfork prong. Cook over hot coals, until done. Serve in a bun with your favorite condiments.

Cooking Food Inside Food

A unique way to both cook and flavor foods is to cook one food inside another. The outer food shields the inner food against the extreme heat and gives additional flavor.

COOKING INSIDE AN ORANGE

Select an orange with a thick peel, because it is easier to remove the fruit inside. Cut the orange in half. Ease your fingers between the flesh and the peel of the orange. Slide your fingers back and forth to detach the flesh from the peel, leaving an orange "cup." A spoon may also help in separating the fruit from the skin. Use the pulp in the next recipe.

Pour cake mix into the orange peel, wrap with foil and cook

Eggs, muffins or cupcakes are all foods which cook nicely inside the peel of an orange. For cupcakes and muffins, fill an orange cup two-thirds full with batter. Place the filled orange cup on a square of aluminum foil. Pull the foil over the cup and twist it at the top to leave room for the food to rise inside the cup. Place on hot coals for about 10 minutes.

Just for fun, cook an egg in one half of the orange and muffin batter in the other half for a quick breakfast. Gingerbread and chocolate cake are also especially delicious this way.

A muffin in one orange peel, an egg in another for a fun breakfast

ORANGE JUICE IN A BAG

Remove the pulp from an orange using the method described on page 89. Place the fruit inside a 1-quart plastic self-sealing bag. Press on both sides of the bag, getting as much air out as you can. Seal the bag. Squeeze the fruit at the bottom to

release all juice. Then turn the bag on its side. Place your hand in the center of the bag on the bottom and loosely gather it to the top, leaving enough room for the juice to flow to the empty side as you continue to squeeze the bottom of the bag. Pop open the top of the bag. Insert a straw where the juice is collecting. Find a

Squeeze your orange in a bag and drink with a straw

log to sit on and continue squeezing the orange. This is the freshest squeezed juice you can have—even made fresher in the brisk outdoor air.

COOKING INSIDE AN ONION

Directions for this method are on pages 58–59, in the foil cooking chapter.

APPLE WALKING SALAD

This is one of my favorites to take on a hike.

2 tablespoons chunky or plain peanut butter
2 tablespoons raisins
1 apple, cored
1 tablespoon lemon juice

In a small bowl, mix peanut butter and raisins. Slice the top off the apple; brush lemon juice onto all cut areas. Spoon mixture into the center and place the top on filled apple. Serves 1.

Apple Walking Salad   *Ants on a Log*

ANTS ON A LOG

A clever snack, especially for kids. These are fun to make and eat, and the flavor is truly delicious.

Celery, cleaned and trimmed
Peanut butter
Raisins

Spread the back of a trimmed length of celery with peanut butter. Place raisins on top of the peanut butter to resemble ants crawling on a "log."

• Cream cheese or a prepared cheese product can be substituted for the peanut butter.

BANANA BOAT

Directions for this delicious recipe are on page 60 in the foil cooking chapter.

SERVING PUDDING CONE

This is a great idea for serving food to children.

1 (3-ounce) package instant pudding, any flavor
Milk
1 ice cream cone per person

Prepare pudding as directed on package. Serve in empty ice cream cones. Top with marshmallows and a cherry if desired. Serves 6 to 8.

• Potato salad, Jell-O, pear halves, and other foods are fun to serve and eat in ice cream cones.

Children of all ages love pudding or pears in a cone

KICK-THE-CAN ICE CREAM

"Ice cream in a tin can" is my most requested recipe. Home-made ice cream is always the most refreshing dessert, and making it outdoors provides both recreation and a cool, memorable treat. It also creates lifetime memories of fun.

1 (1-pound) coffee can with plastic lid
1 cup whole milk
1 cup heavy cream
1/3 cup sugar
2 tablespoons flavored syrup (such as chocolate or
    strawberry)
1 (3-pound) coffee can with plastic lid or a #10-size can,
    such as a potato flake can with plastic lid
Small bag ice, cubed (not crushed)
1/2 cup rock salt

In the small can, add milk, cream, sugar and syrup. Do not fill the can more than half full with liquids or the ice cream will not freeze as well. Cover the small can with a plastic lid and place it into the large can. Fill the bottom half of the space between the two cans with ice. Add rock salt. Fill the rest of the space with ice and put on the plastic lid.

Ask two people to roll the can back and forth to each other for 10 minutes. (You might want to set a timer because small children have little concept of time.) Remove the lids and scrape the ice cream from the sides of the small can. Stir the mixture. If the ice cream needs to freeze longer, pour water out of the large can. Set the small can inside the large can, adding more ice and rock salt as needed. When the ice cream is ready, there will be about a half inch of frozen mixture on the sides of the can, the rest still in near-liquid form. With a kitchen knife scrape down the frozen ice cream and stir it into the liquid ice cream to create the right consistency. Makes about 2 cups.

• Chopped frozen fruit may be added with the syrup if desired. It also speeds freezing.

Kick-the-Can Ice Cream, a frozen treat made in a tin can

BALL TOSS ICE CREAM

This is a great group activity for kids. Divide into pairs and make one recipe per pair. To make 2 cups you will need:

1 cup whole milk
1 cup heavy cream
1/3 cup sugar
2 (1-quart) plastic self-sealing bags
2 (1-gallon) plastic self-sealing bags
1/2 cup rock salt
Ice, cubed (not crushed)
Newspapers
Duct tape

In a 1-quart plastic self-sealing bag, combine milk, cream and sugar. Squeeze as much air out of the bag as you can. Close the bag and place it inside another 1-quart plastic self-sealing bag. (It is double-bagged for strength.) Set the ice cream mixture into the 1-gallon plastic self-sealing bag. Fill the area between with ice and rock salt, alternately. Seal the bag. Put this bag inside a second 1-gallon bag.

Open up sections of newspaper as if you were reading the center pages. Stack the newspapers on top of each other until you have a half-inch-high stack. Place the ice cream package in a corner of the papers. Lift the corner and roll the whole package again until you have covered the entire package with newspaper. Fold in both sides and continue rolling the ice cream package. Repeat until all newspapers are used. Tape the newspapers shut with duct tape. Secure the "ball" on all sides so that it will retain its shape when tossed. Each pair of kids can toss the "ice cream ball" back and forth for 15 to 20 minutes. Makes about 2 cups.

TIN CAN STOVE

One of the most innovative outdoor cooking methods, and excellent to have for power-related emergencies at home, is the simple homemade tin can stove which can be used for frying, boiling and toasting. It is best used for one or two people because of its small size. It is also disposable; just recycle after use.

A buddy burner (a tuna can—or a can similar in shape—filled with rolled corrugated cardboard and melted paraffin) is the main source of heat for a tin can stove.

To make the tin can stove:

First, cut out one end of the #10-size can (102-ounce or 6-pound 6-ounce) available from restaurants. With tin snips cut two slits 3 inches high and 3 1/2 inches apart on one side of the can at the open end, leaving the top attached. Pull the door open. With a punch-type can opener, punch two or three holes on the backside of the can near the top. These act as a chimney, allowing the smoke to escape during cooking.

A skillet may be used on top of the tin can by removing the top so it is open. When using pans, be sure to rub liquid soap on the bottom of the pan so they will clean easily.

Cut top from #10-size can to cook with a frying pan

To make the buddy burner:

Cut corrugated cardboard (across the corrugation so holes show) into strips the same width as the height of the tuna can. Roll strips tightly to fit inside the can. Heat the wax in a **double boiler** and pour melted wax into the cardboard. Or set a piece of wax on the cardboard and light a match next to the wax (see picture). Continue adding wax near the flame until the buddy burner is filled. The cardboard serves as a wick, and the wax serves as the fuel, providing the heat for the stove.

When lighting, it may help to lay the can on its side so that the flame spreads across the cardboard. It will burn 1 1/2 to 2 hours. To refuel, add a new small piece of wax when it is burning and let it melt into the burner. When finished, let the wax harden before storing.

Use a tuna can, wax and cardboard to make the buddy burner

To make the damper:

A damper covers the buddy burner to control the amount of heat. It is easy to make out of foil or from the lid of a tuna can. To make: fold an 18-inch by 15-inch piece of heavy-duty foil into 3-inch sections again and again until all the foil is used. Bend the foil down as a handle to set over the tuna can. To make a handle with a cardboard pant hanger (minus the cardboard), bend ends together. Punch holes in the top of the tuna can lid on each side. Wire the lid to the ends of the hanger. Bend the handle of the coat hanger down so that it will prop itself up while the buddy burner is burning. Move the damper to increase or decrease the heat. (On page 95 you will see damper made from tuna lid and pant hanger.)

BOILING WATER IN A PAPER CUP

It is possible to **boil water** in an unwaxed paper cup without the cup igniting. Pour water or milk into the cup. Cut a small square of aluminum foil and place it under the cup. Set foil and cup in or on the hot coals. The foil protects the small lip on the bottom from burning. If flames rise against the top of the cup where liquid does not reach, the cup can burn.

Another way to boil **water** in a paper cup is to place the cup on a buddy burner (see buddy burner on page 96). If water happens to seep out, or if the rim of the cup that extends below the

It sounds impossible, but YES! You can boil water in a paper cup

bottom starts to drip, pour the water into a different cup and repeat. You will be amazed to see water actually boiling. Stir in ingredients to create your favorite hot beverage such as hot chocolate.

You can hard-cook eggs in a paper cup. It is also possible to heat a carton of **milk** if the carton is unwaxed. Open the milk carton top before heating.

BREAKFAST COOKED IN A PAPER BAG

To cook bacon and eggs for breakfast, cut a strip of bacon in half. Spread it in the bottom of a new lunch-sized paper sack. Break an egg and drop it on top of the bacon inside the sack. To make scrambled eggs, open and fold down the top of the bag. Crack the shell, hold it high over the bag, and release the egg. When it hits the bottom of the bag, it will be scrambled.

Beginning at the top, roll the sack down in one-inch folds until you reach the middle of the sack. Poke a stick through the rolled folds at the top of the sack and hold it over a bed of coals or set it on a piece of foil above a bed of hot coals. Grease will appear along the bottom of the bag as the food cooks. The bacon and egg will cook in approximately 10 minutes.

This is also easy to cook on a tin can stove. During the last two minutes before eggs are done, place two slices of white

Eggs and bacon in a paper bag with toast "on the side"

sandwich bread on either side of the can. If the can is very hot, the bread will stick to the can. Wait a few minutes and pop the toasted bread off with a spatula or a hot pad to prevent burns (see photo above).

LEAF COOKING

Another quick and easy "utensil" for cooking ground beef is a cabbage leaf used as a pan. Shape a ground beef patty, set it on the leaf and place the leaf directly onto the hot coals. The edges of the leaf will turn brown, but the center remains firm. With a spatula and a hot pad turn the meat over on the leaf halfway through the cooking time.

CHAPTER 7

Breakfasts

There's nothing to equal the smell of fresh smoked bacon cooking over an outdoor fire as the sun comes up in the quiet, crisp morning against nature's backdrop. Many outdoor cooks have not experimented with breakfast foods beyond the basics. My recipes combine the best of breakfast items with easy ideas to make convenient, delicious and nutritious breakfasts out of doors. One of my favorites is the aptly named **Sunshine Toast** (page 102), a combination of eggs, bacon and French toast.

A nourishing morning meal is the most important meal of the day. Children are even more active outdoors, and a good breakfast keeps their energy level high. These breakfast ideas were designed to offer easy yet nourishing meals to start the day out right.

Ready-to-Eat and Prepared Foods

- Cold cereals
- Granola
- Instant cream of wheat
- Instant grits
- Instant oatmeal

Toppings:

- Brown sugar
- Honey
- Syrup

Dairy and nondairy:

- Cream
- Evaporated milk
- Half and half
- Milk
- Sweetened condensed milk
- Yogurt

EGGS, BACON, SAUSAGE AND HAM

The smell of bacon, sausage and ham cooking on your camp stove is the most perfect way to begin the day.

Camp Stove and At Home

To cook breakfast on a camp stove or range, you will use a frying pan or griddle to cook eggs, bacon, sausage and ham. Cook bacon, sausage or ham slowly on the low setting, turning often to brown. Remove from pan, set aside and pour off all but 1 tablespoon of drippings. Add eggs and cook as desired.

Dutch Oven

Heat a 12-inch Dutch oven over 12 to 15 hot coals. Fry bacon, sausage or ham, turning often to brown. Remove from oven, set aside and pour off all but 1 tablespoon of drippings. Add eggs and cook as desired.

Dutch Oven Lid

Place the lid of a 12-inch Dutch oven upside down on a lid holder and follow the above **Dutch oven** directions.

- Always keep eggs chilled in a refrigerator or cooler until cooked.

• Plastic egg holders are available to keep eggs from breaking during transport. Avoid using cracked eggs.

About Eggs—

Always refrigerate eggs. If stored at room temperature, they lose more quality in one day than a week in the refrigerator. Store in the carton they came in; an open egg container exposes them to odors and damage. The best flavor will be realized if they are

Handle your eggs with care in a plastic egg holder

used within a week. Hard-cooked eggs should be kept no more than one week. Used in recipes, eggs provide leavening for cakes, breads and soufflés; a base for dressings such as mayonnaise; a thickener in sauces and custard; a clarifying agent for stocks; a coating for breaded or battered foods; and a binder when used with cereal in ground beef combinations.

PANCAKES

The easiest way to make pancakes outdoors is to use a commercial mix.

Foods you can add to pancake batter are:

- Bananas and other fruits
- Blueberries
- Chocolate chips

- Chopped nuts
- Cranberries, dried
- Currants, dried
- Raisins
- Raspberries

Toppings:

- Fruit-flavored syrup
- Jams, jellies and marmalades
- Lemon, lime and orange curd

- Maple syrup
- Pie fillings
- Powdered sugar
- Whipped cream, pressurized can

SUNSHINE TOAST

My all-time, most-often-cooked recipe. I love to cook it on a tin can stove.

4 slices bacon
4 slices bread
4 eggs
1/2 teaspoon salt
1/4 teaspoon pepper

Camp Stove and At Home

In a large frying pan, fold bacon strips into "V's." Cook on one side and turn over. Tear a hole in the center of the bread slice large enough to hold an egg. Place the bread slice onto the bacon, and break an egg in the center of the bread hole. Season with salt and pepper. When the egg is done on one side, turn over and cook to desired doneness. Serves 4.

• For eggs and bacon on one side and French toast on the other, with a fork scramble the egg and draw from the center over the bread. Turn over to cook the French toast. You now have **eggs and bacon on one side and French toast on the other.**

Sunshine toast cooked on a tin can stove is sure to become a favorite of yours, too

CRUNCHY FRENCH TOAST

A delicious recipe your family will love! The flavors stay with you long after breakfast is over.

4 eggs
1 cup heavy cream or milk
1/4 teaspoon salt
1/8 teaspoon pepper
8 (1-inch-thick) slices French bread
1 tablespoon oil
1 tablespoon butter or margarine
1 cup maple syrup

In a 1-gallon plastic self-sealing bag, mix eggs, cream, salt and pepper. Add bread slices to the bag and turn over to soak the liquid.

Camp Stove and At Home

Heat a large frying pan; add oil and butter. When hot, arrange pieces of soaked bread. Cook on both sides until golden brown. Serve with syrup. Serves 4.

Dutch Oven

Heat a 12-inch Dutch oven over 12 to 15 hot coals. Melt oil and butter in Dutch oven and arrange bread slices in pan. Cook on both sides until golden brown. Serve with syrup. Serves 4.

Dutch Oven Lid

Place the lid of a 12-inch Dutch oven upside down on a lid holder over 12 to 15 hot coals and follow the above **Dutch oven** directions.

- Topping variations might include:
  - Cinnamon sugar
  - Honey
  - Jams, jellies or marmalades
  - Powdered sugar
  - Sugar

BREAKFAST QUESADILLAS

Great for a snack as well as for lunch or dinner—and they are delicious.

    8 (8-inch) flour tortillas
    2 to 3 tablespoons oil
    3 to 4 cups Cheddar cheese, shredded
    16 ham slices, thinly sliced
    1 cup green onions, thinly sliced
    1 cup sour cream
    1 cup salsa

• Sliced jalapeño peppers can be added, if desired.

Camp Stove and At Home

Heat a large frying pan. Brush 2 tortillas with oil on one side. Place one tortilla, oiled side down, in the pan. Add 1/2 cup cheese, 2 slices of ham and a few slices of green onion. Cover with another tortilla, oiled side up. Cook on medium heat until bottom tortilla is crisp on the bottom. Turn over and cook until cheese is melted and the bottom is crisp. Repeat as needed. Cut into wedges and serve with sour cream and salsa. Serves 6 to 8.

Grill

Set grill temperature at the lowest possible setting. Brush 2 tortillas with oil on one side. Set one tortilla, oiled side down, on the grill. Add 1/2 cup cheese, 2 slices of ham and a few slices of green onion. Cover with another tortilla, oiled side up. Grill a few minutes until crisp on the bottom. Turn over and grill until cheese has melted and the bottom is crisp. Repeat as needed. Cut into wedges and serve with sour cream and salsa. Serves 6 to 8.

Dutch Oven

Heat a 12-inch Dutch oven over 12 to 15 hot coals. When very hot, brush with oil. Brush 2 tortillas with oil on one side, and place one tortilla, oiled side down, in the Dutch oven. Add 1/2 cup cheese, 2 slices of ham and a few slices of green onion. Cover with another tortilla, oiled side up. Cook until crisp on the bottom. Turn over and cook until the cheese has melted and the bottom is crisp. Repeat as needed. Cut into wedges and serve with sour cream and salsa. Serves 6 to 8.

Dutch Oven Lid

Place a 12-inch Dutch oven lid upside down on a lid holder and follow the above directions for **Dutch oven** method.

• Fry or scramble eggs to add between the cheese and ham for an instant breakfast sandwich.

CHILI AND CHEESE OMELET

3 tablespoons olive oil
2 (6-ounce) cans whole chili peppers
6 eggs, beaten
1/4 teaspoon salt
1 pinch cayenne pepper
1/2 cup Monterey Jack cheese, shredded

Camp Stove and At Home

In a large skillet, heat the oil and sauté the peppers for 1 to 2 minutes. Pour eggs over peppers and turn heat to low. Cook, covered, until eggs are desired doneness. Sprinkle with salt, pepper and cheese. Cut into squares to serve. Serves 3 to 4.

• *Sauté* means to "jump" or quickly stir food in a small amount of butter or oil over direct heat until soft.

HARD-COOKED EGGS

Eggs, as needed
Water, as needed

Camp Stove and At Home

In a medium saucepan, add eggs and cover with water. Bring to a boil. Cover with a lid and remove from the heat. Do not lift the lid for 15 to 20 minutes.

VEGETABLE FRITTATA

A *frittata* is an Italian omelet that mixes all ingredients into the eggs during cooking. The entire omelet may be turned over after ingredients are partially cooked instead of folded in half.

1/4 cup oil
1 zucchini, thinly sliced
1 small onion, thinly sliced
1/4 teaspoon salt
1/8 teaspoon pepper
6 eggs, beaten
1 cup Cheddar cheese, shredded

Camp Stove and At Home

In a large frying pan on medium-low, heat oil; add zucchini and onion in one layer, covering the bottom of the pan. Cook for 10 to 15 minutes, on low heat, until vegetables are soft and browning occurs. Season with salt and pepper.

Pour eggs over the zucchini and onion and cook until the bottom starts to brown. (You can "flip" the frittata over, if desired.) Sprinkle the cheese on top and cover. When egg is thoroughly cooked and the cheese is melted, cut into wedges and serve immediately. Serves 4.

Dutch Oven

Heat a 12-inch Dutch oven over 12 to 15 hot coals and add oil. Arrange the zucchini and onion in one layer covering the bottom of the Dutch oven. Cook for 10 to 15 minutes, until vegetables are soft and browning occurs. Sprinkle with salt and pepper.

Pour eggs on the zucchini and onion and cook until the bottom starts to brown. (You can flip the frittata over, if desired.) Sprinkle the cheese on top and cover. When egg is thoroughly cooked and the cheese is melted, cut into wedges and serve immediately. Serves 4.

• Sliced avocado and tomatoes may be added to the beaten eggs or served as a garnish.

• A large pan of eggs may be difficult to "flip over." Covering with a lid will thoroughly cook the eggs.

BRIGHTEN-UP BREAKFAST

1/2 pound bacon, diced
1 (29-ounce) can potatoes or 4 medium precooked
    potatoes, cubed
1/2 teaspoon salt
1/8 teaspoon pepper
6 eggs

Camp Stove and At Home

In a large skillet, fry bacon. Pour off all but 2 tablespoons of drippings. Add potatoes and season with salt and pepper. Cook, turning occasionally, until golden brown. Remove from pan and set aside. In the pan, add more drippings if needed and scramble the eggs as desired. Serve warm with potatoes. Serves 4.

Dutch Oven

Heat a 12-inch Dutch oven over 12 to 15 hot coals and fry bacon. Pour off all but 2 tablespoons of the drippings. Add potatoes and season with salt and pepper. Cook, stirring occasionally, until golden brown. Remove from the pan and set aside. In the pan, add more drippings if needed and scramble the eggs as desired. Serve warm with potatoes. Serves 4.

• Precook potatoes until tender at home. A microwave oven does this well. Place in a plastic self-sealing bag and keep in the refrigerator or cooler until ready to use.

• For **campfire potatoes**, wrap oiled potatoes in aluminum foil and place near the side of hot coals. Cook for 30 minutes on one side. Turn over and leave overnight.

CORNED BEEF HASH

2 tablespoons oil
1 (1-pound) can corned beef, diced
4 medium potatoes, cooked, peeled, and diced
1 small onion, minced
1 egg, beaten
1/2 teaspoon salt
1/8 teaspoon pepper

Camp Stove and At Home

In a large frying pan, heat oil. In a large mixing bowl, combine corned beef, potatoes, onion, egg, salt and pepper, and shape into patties (about 3 inches in diameter and 1/2-inch thick). Cook patties on both sides until crispy and browned. Serves 4 to 6.

Dutch Oven

Heat a 12-inch Dutch oven over 12 to 15 hot coals until very hot. In a large mixing bowl, combine corned beef, potatoes, onion, egg, salt and pepper, and shape into patties (about 3 inches in diameter and 1/2-inch thick). Heat oil and cook patties in Dutch oven on both sides until crispy and browned. Serves 4 to 6.

• Canned or leftover boiled or baked potatoes can be substituted for fresh.

• You may substitute 3 cups of diced, cooked ham or beef for the corned beef.

SAUSAGE AND HOME FRIES

1 pound breakfast sausage links, cut into 1-inch sections
1 medium onion, minced
4 medium potatoes, cooked and cubed
1/2 teaspoon salt
1/8 teaspoon pepper
2 cups Cheddar cheese, shredded

Camp Stove and At Home

In a large frying pan, sauté sausage until half-cooked. Add onion and potatoes, stirring frequently, until golden brown. Salt and pepper. Sprinkle cheese on top and cover. Serve when cheese is melted. Serves 4.

Dutch Oven

Heat a 12-inch Dutch oven over 12 to 15 hot coals. Sauté sausage in the Dutch oven until half-cooked. Add onion and potatoes, stirring frequently, until golden brown. Salt and pepper. Sprinkle cheese on top and cover. Serve when cheese is melted. Serves 4.

JOHNNY CAKES

Howard Helmer, the Egg King, shared this delicious recipe with me in my home.

6 eggs
1 (8.5-ounce) package corn muffin mix
1 (8-ounce) can whole-kernel corn, drained
1 cup filling (see •)
1 teaspoon cooking oil
1 cup sour cream
1 cup salsa

• Filling suggestions for Johnny Cakes are 1/2 to 1 cup of any of the following: chopped ham, diced cooked bacon, thinly sliced green onions, mushrooms, or red or green peppers, or a combination of several.

Camp Stove and At Home

In a small mixing bowl, beat eggs until foamy and add unprepared muffin mix until thoroughly blended. Add corn and desired fillings, blending well. In a large frying pan on medium, heat oil. Spoon about 1/4 cup of batter into the hot pan for each cake. When bubbles appear at edges, turn over and cook until lightly browned. Serve with sour cream and salsa. Serves 4.

CEREAL PORRIDGE

A healthy and hearty breakfast, especially welcome on a cool morning. For a hot cereal, you won't believe how good this is!

   6 cups water
   1/3 teaspoon salt
   3 cups rolled grain of oats, rye, wheat, barley, or any combination
   1/2 cup shelled sunflower seeds
   1/2 cup dried fruit such as prunes, apricots, figs, currants, or raisins, chopped
   1/2 cup walnuts, chopped
   1 tablespoon lemon or orange zest, finely shredded
   1 quart milk or heavy cream
   1 cup brown sugar

Camp Stove and At Home

In a large saucepan, boil water and salt; stir in rolled grains. Cook, stirring occasionally, for 10 minutes. Cover, turn off the heat and let it rest for 20 minutes. Add sunflower seeds, fruit, nuts and zest of orange or lemon. Stir and serve with milk or cream and brown sugar. Serves 4 to 6.

Dutch Oven

Heat a 12-inch Dutch oven over 12 to 15 hot coals. Boil water and salt; stir in rolled grains. Cook, stirring occasionally, for 10 minutes. Cover, move away from the coals and let it rest for 20 minutes. Add sunflower seeds, fruit, nuts and zest of orange or lemon. Stir and serve with milk or cream and brown sugar. Serves 4 to 6.

CHAPTER 8

Soups and Stews

O ur connection with the past and to our ancestors comes alive whenever soups, stews and other old-fashioned one-pot meals are served. When it's comfort food we're looking for, these recipes always hit the spot. And with today's convenient ingredients, these old-time favorites are made easily and in less time than most of us imagine.

Soups and stews are an excellent way of combining assorted foods from different food groups. Because they are slow-cooked in liquid, you can enjoy the view without tending the fire so closely. Their heartiness makes them perfect for the outdoors. Perhaps you've never thought of something so elaborate or delicious as **French Onion Soup** (page 114) but I've included an easy recipe that's perfect for outside dining.

Ready-to-Eat and Prepared Foods

Few things are more convenient while camping than premade soup that just needs warming. Dried or canned soups from supermarkets are excellent served plain or combined with other ingredients for a heartier meal. Some soups come in cups and require only adding hot water.

Soups in a cup:

- Bean
- Black bean
- Chicken vegetable
- Corn chowder
- Couscous
- Hearty lentil
- Lentil
- Navy bean
- Potato leek
- Rice and vegetable
- Split pea
- Vegetarian vegetable

Bouillon cubes or canned broths:

- Beef
- Chicken
- Fish
- Vegetarian or meatless

Packaged soups:

- Cream of broccoli
- Creamy chicken and rice
- French onion
- Leek
- Oxtail
- Roasted garlic herb
- Spinach
- Spring vegetable
- Tomato basil
- Vegetable

Convenient Combinations

The number of servings for the following recipes varies by the amount of ingredients added.

CREAMY CHEESE AND BROCCOLI SOUP

Cook 1 (10-ounce) package of frozen chopped broccoli until tender. Add 1 (11.5-ounce) can Cheddar cheese soup and 1 cup of heavy cream or milk. Heat and serve. Serves 3 to 4.

CHICKEN AND RICE SOUP

Combine 1 (14.5-ounce) can chicken broth and 1 cup instant brown rice. Cook for 2 to 3 minutes and add 1 (10-ounce) can chicken and 1 (11.5-ounce) can cream of chicken soup, diluted with heavy cream or evaporated milk, if necessary. Heat and serve. Serves 3 to 4.

OYSTER STEW

Combine 1 (6-ounce) can cooked oysters, 1 (11.5-ounce) can cream of mushroom soup and 1 cup heavy cream or evaporated milk. Heat thoroughly and serve with oyster crackers. Serves 3 to 4.

SHEEPHERDER'S STEW

1 pound ground beef
1/2 onion, diced
1/2 teaspoon salt
4 potatoes, peeled and diced
2 to 3 carrots, peeled and diced
2 (11.5-ounce) cans cream of mushroom soup
1 cup milk

Camp Stove and At Home

In a large fry pan on medium heat, combine ground beef and onion, stirring to brown. Add salt, potatoes and carrots. Cook for 5 minutes. Add soup and milk. Cook, covered, on low heat until vegetables are tender, about 25 minutes. Serves 4 to 6.

Dutch Oven

Heat a 12-inch Dutch oven over 9 hot coals. Add ground beef and onion, stirring to brown. Add salt, potatoes, and carrots. Cook for 5 minutes. Add soup and milk. Cover and place 15 hot coals on the top; cook until vegetables are tender, about 25 minutes. Serves 4 to 6.

• Ground lamb or turkey may be substituted for beef.

FRENCH ONION SOUP

3 tablespoons butter or margarine
3 large onions, sliced
3 tablespoons all-purpose flour
1 cup white wine, optional
6 cups beef broth
1 bouquet garni (page 176)
12 slices baguette, toasted
6 ounces Gruyère cheese, shredded

Camp Stove and At Home

In a 2-quart saucepan, melt the butter. Add onions and cook until golden brown, about 20 minutes. Stir in flour and cook for 1 to 2 minutes, stirring well. Add wine, broth and bouquet garni. Simmer, covered, for at least 1 hour.

Place 1 or 2 slices of baguette in each soup bowl and sprinkle shredded cheese on top. Pour hot soup on the bread and cheese. Serve immediately. Serves 6 to 8.

Dutch Oven

Heat a 12-inch Dutch oven over 12 to 15 hot coals. Melt the butter and add onions, cooking until golden brown, about 20 minutes. Stir in flour and cook for 1 to 2 minutes, stirring well. Add wine, broth and bouquet garni. Simmer, covered, for at least 1 hour.

Place 1 or 2 slices of baguette in each soup bowl and top with shredded cheese. Pour hot soup on the bread and cheese. Serve immediately. Serves 6 to 8.

BACON AND CORN CHOWDER

4 slices bacon, diced
1 medium onion, minced
6 medium potatoes, peeled and cubed
2 cups chicken broth
2 (15-ounce) cans creamed corn
1 cup heavy cream or milk
1/2 teaspoon salt
1/2 teaspoon pepper

Camp Stove and At Home

In a 2-quart saucepan on medium heat, sauté bacon and onion. Pour off drippings. Add potatoes and cook for 10 minutes. Add broth and corn; cook, stirring occasionally, for 40 minutes, until potatoes are tender. Add cream, salt and pepper, and heat until hot. Serves 6 to 8.

Dutch Oven

Heat a 12-inch Dutch oven over 12 to 15 hot coals. Sauté bacon and onion. Pour off drippings. Add potatoes and cook for 10 minutes. Add broth and corn; cook, stirring occasionally, for 40 minutes, until potatoes are tender. Add cream, salt and pepper, and heat until hot. Serves 6 to 8.

• Ham hocks or smoked ham may be substituted for bacon.

BROCCOLI SOUP

2 cups chicken broth
2 cups heavy cream or milk
2 cups milk
4 cups broccoli, cooked
1 teaspoon onion powder
4 tablespoons beurre manie (see •)
3 cups sharp Cheddar cheese, shredded
1/2 teaspoon salt
1/4 teaspoon pepper

• *Beurre manie* is a prepared paste of equal parts softened butter and flour used to thicken sauces. It can be premade and stored, covered, in the refrigerator for use whenever a sauce needs reducing or thickening. These are the correct proportions for a medium white sauce.

Camp Stove and At Home

In a 3-quart saucepan, heat broth, cream and milk. Add broccoli and onion powder and bring to a boil. Stir in the beurre manie and blend until smooth. Add cheese, salt and pepper. Serve when cheese is melted. Serves 6 to 8.

Dutch Oven

Heat a 12-inch Dutch oven over 12 to 15 hot coals. Add broth, cream and milk. Add broccoli and onion powder and bring to a boil. Stir in the beurre manie and blend until smooth. Add cheese, salt and pepper. Serve when cheese is melted. Serves 6 to 8.

CHILI AND CHEESE HOT POT

3 (15-ounce) cans chili with beans
1 (7-ounce) can whole green chilies, cut into strips
3 cups beef broth
1 cup Cheddar or Monterey Jack cheese, shredded
1 small onion, chopped
1/2 cup sour cream

Camp Stove and At Home

In a 3-quart saucepan, heat chili, green chilies and broth until hot, about 20 minutes. Divide into 4 to 6 soup bowls and add cheese, onions and sour cream to the top of each bowl. Serves 4 to 6.

Dutch Oven

Heat a 12-inch Dutch oven over 12 to 15 hot coals. Heat chili, green chilies and broth until hot, about 20 to 30 minutes. Divide into 4 to 6 soup bowls and top each bowl with cheese, onions and sour cream. Serves 4 to 6.

ASPARAGUS WITH SHRIMP SOUP

3 (11.5-ounce) cans cream of asparagus soup
1 1/2 cups milk
1/2 cup heavy cream or milk
2 (6-ounce) cans broken or tiny shrimp
1/2 cup green onions, chopped

Camp Stove and At Home

In a 3-quart saucepan, heat soup, milk and cream, stirring constantly, until hot. Add shrimp and green onions and let it rest, covered, a few minutes before serving in individual bowls. Serves 4 to 6.

Dutch Oven

Heat a 12-inch Dutch oven over 12 to 15 hot coals. Add soup, milk and cream, stirring constantly, until hot. Add shrimp and green onions and let it rest, covered, a few minutes before serving in individual bowls. Serves 4 to 6.

• Cream of celery soup may be substituted for cream of asparagus soup.

PUMPKIN, LIME AND GINGER SOUP

1 (29-ounce) can pure pumpkin

2 (12-ounce) cans evaporated milk

3 (15-ounce) cans chicken broth

1/2 cup lime juice

2 tablespoons fresh ginger, shredded

1 tablespoon honey

Camp Stove and At Home

In a 3-quart saucepan, combine pumpkin, milk, broth, lime juice, ginger and honey. Heat, stirring constantly, for 10 minutes. Simmer another 10 to 20 minutes to blend flavors. Serves 6 to 8.

• This soup also tastes scrumptious made with squash instead of pumpkin. Cook 4 cups of cubed squash until soft; drain, mash and use as you would the canned pumpkin.

TOMATO SOUP ELEGANTÉ

3 (11.5-ounce) cans tomato soup, undiluted

1 cup chicken broth

1 cup heavy cream or milk

Camp Stove and At Home

In a 3-quart saucepan, combine soup, broth and cream. Cook, stirring constantly, until steaming hot, about 8 to 10 minutes. Serves 4.

• Any chopped vegetables, chives or a dollop of sour cream make a great garnish for this soup.

CHAPTER 9

Salads

Too often our limited thinking of salads begins and ends with lettuce. There are so many delicious vegetables, fruits, nuts, grains and other foods that can adapt a simple salad into an entire meal. Successful salad secrets depend on your creativity or a good recipe book. One of my favorite ideas for outdoors is a **Fruit Pudding Salad** (page 121) made from canned and/or fresh fruit using instant lemon pudding for a zesty, flavorful dressing.

Creativity in the presentation enhances a salad or vegetable snack. Let your imagination guide you. I prepare and serve salads in 1-gallon plastic self-sealing bags inside a 3-pound coffee can or #10-size can. Open the top of the bag and rest it on the rim of the can for easy serving. For a raw vegetable snack outdoors, in the bottom of a plastic cup or paper cup place dip or ranch dressing and add carrots and celery strips to create a **"Stand-Up" Salad** (see photo on back cover).

Ready-to-Eat and Prepared Foods

Salads are easier to make than ever because greens are available from the grocery store cleaned, snipped into bite-sized pieces, and ready to serve.

Packaged salads include:

- Baby spinach
- Caesar salad mix
- Classic mix
- Cole slaw mix
- European mix
- Romaine mix

Suggested condiments:

- Artichoke hearts
- Black olives
- Cheeses
- Chicken pouches
- Chopped ham
- Fruits such as cantaloupe, apples, oranges, etc.
- Green olives
- Hard-cooked eggs
- Meats
- Pickled asparagus
- Pickles
- Three-bean salad
- Tuna pouches

Dressings are available in many varieties. Plastic bottles and squeeze tubes are great for camping trips.

Classics:

- Bleu cheese
- French
- Italian
- Oil and vinegar
- Ranch
- Thousand Island

ITALIAN GREEN BEAN SALAD

1 bag Romaine or Caesar mixed greens
2 (15-ounce) cans whole green beans, drained
1 (15-ounce) can marinated olives, drained
Italian dressing

In a salad bowl, combine greens, green beans and olives. Add dressing, as desired. Serves 4 to 6.

FRUIT PUDDING SALAD

This recipe is a snap to make and may be either a salad or a dessert. Children request it often, so they can help.

1 (1-pound 4-ounce) can pineapple chunks with juice
2 bananas, peeled and sliced
1 (11-ounce) can mandarin oranges, drained
1 (15-ounce) can fruit cocktail with juice
1 cup shredded coconut
1 (3 3/4-ounce) package instant lemon pudding mix

In a medium bowl, combine pineapple chunks and juice with bananas, oranges, fruit cocktail with juice, and coconut. Stirring slowly, sprinkle pudding mix into fruit mixture. Let it rest 5 minutes, or until set. Serves 6 to 8.

• Open a 1-gallon plastic self-sealing bag and ease it into a 3-pound coffee can or a #10-size can. Prepare the above recipe in the bag, push most of the air out and seal; mix with your hands, squeezing the bag. Place bag into the can, unzip and serve. Serves 6 to 8.

Enjoy the refreshing pudding salad

VEGETABLE AND RICE SALAD

1 (12-ounce) package frozen or fully cooked rice or risotto, thawed
2 cups fresh broccoli, finely chopped
2 hard-cooked eggs, chopped
Vinaigrette dressing, your choice (page 184)

In a salad bowl, combine rice, broccoli and eggs. Add dressing, as desired. Serves 4 to 6.

GARBANZO SALAD

2 (15-ounce) cans garbanzo beans, drained
1 small onion, sliced
1/4 cup fresh parsley, minced
Lemon vinaigrette dressing (page 185)

In a salad bowl, combine garbanzo beans, onion and parsley. Add dressing, as desired. Serves 4 to 6.

CORN SALAD

2 (15-ounce) cans whole-kernel corn, drained, or kernels from 8 cooked ears
1/4 cup onion, minced
1 cup zucchini, cut into thin matchstick strips
1 cup carrots, cut into thin matchstick strips
1/2 cup lemon vinaigrette dressing (page 185)

In a salad bowl, combine corn, onion, zucchini and carrots. Add dressing, as desired. Serves 4 to 6.

DANDELION GREENS WITH SMOKED HAM

When the "troops" run out of things to do, send them out to pick dandelions. Use the flowers for a centerpiece and the greens for this salad.

3 cups dandelion greens or mixed salad greens
1/2 red onion, sliced
1/2 cup smoked ham, cubed
1 cup bleu cheese or Roquefort dressing

Wash greens thoroughly and pat dry with paper towels. In a salad bowl, tear greens into bite-sized pieces and combine with onion, smoked ham and dressing, as desired. Serves 4 to 6.

• In the woods dandelions probably haven't been sprayed with insecticide; however, avoid using those in your yard that might have been sprayed.

POTATO SALAD à la FRANCE

12 small red or white potatoes, cooked and cooled
1/3 cup white wine, optional
1/3 cup chicken broth
1 green onion, minced
1/4 cup parsley, minced
1/2 teaspoon salt
1/4 teaspoon pepper
2/3 cup champagne vinaigrette dressing (page 186)

Into a large salad bowl, peel and slice potatoes. Sprinkle with combined wine and broth. Serve at room temperature topped with green onion, parsley, salt, pepper and vinaigrette dressing. Serves 4 to 6.

• A small amount of vinegar or lemon juice may be substituted for the wine.

TOMATO AND MARINATED CHEESE SALAD

Home-grown tomatoes from a garden are always more flavorful (unless you can buy hot-house tomatoes).

1 pound cheese such as feta, fontina or Havarti
1 cup marinade for cheese (page 181)
6 ripe tomatoes, thinly sliced
1 small onion, sliced
3 tablespoons fresh chives or 1 tablespoon dried chives

In a 1-gallon plastic self-sealing bag, marinate cheese overnight or for 2 to 3 days (or even up to a week, if desired). On a large flat platter, arrange tomatoes. Cut or crumble marinated cheese and sprinkle onto tomatoes. Pour marinade on top, covering all tomatoes. Decorate with onion rings and chives. Serves 4.

RICE SALAD

A delicious one-dish meal served hot or cold.

    1/2 cup mayonnaise
    1/4 cup dill pickle juice
    1 large dill pickle, minced
    4 cups rice, cooked and cooled
    2 (7-ounce) cans tuna, drained
    4 hard-cooked eggs, chopped
    2 tomatoes, cut into wedges
    1/2 small onion, minced
    2 to 3 green onions, sliced
    1 cup black olives, halved

In a small bowl, mix mayonnaise with the pickle juice and set aside. In a medium salad bowl, combine dill pickle, rice, tuna, eggs, tomatoes, onion, green onions and olives. Add mayonnaise mixture, blending well. Serves 4 to 6.

MARINATED STEAK ON MIXED GREENS

    1 pound sirloin steak
    1 cup marinade for beef (page 182)
    3 cups mixed greens
    1 ripe tomato, diced
    1 small onion, sliced
    1 ripe avocado, peeled and sliced
    1/2 cup black olives, halved
    1 cup balsamic vinaigrette dressing (page 184)

Grill and At Home

In a 1-gallon plastic self-sealing bag, marinate steak overnight. Pat it dry with paper towels and place on a hot oiled grill. Cook 5 to 10 minutes on each side, depending on the degree of doneness you desire. (See page 73 for meat temperature chart.) Remove the steak from the grill and let it rest 5 minutes. Slice very thinly on the diagonal across the grain.

In a large salad bowl, mix greens, tomato, onion, avocado and olives, and arrange sliced steak on top. Drizzle with salad dressing and serve. Serves 4 to 6.

SLICED BEET SALAD

2 (15-ounce) cans sliced beets, drained
4 green onions, sliced
2 hard-cooked eggs, sliced
1/2 cup basic vinaigrette dressing (page 184)

On a large platter, arrange beets. Decorate with green onions and egg slices and drizzle with vinaigrette. Serves 6 to 8.

PASTA SALAD

Pasta salads are an easy main dish because the vegetables, meats and pasta are combined. They are also great to make ahead for entertaining.

4 quarts water
2 cups dry pasta, such as fuselli or rotelli
1 (8-ounce) bottle Caesar salad dressing (see •)
1 cup fresh Parmesan cheese, shredded
1 cup mixed vegetables (tomatoes, carrots, broccoli, chives, etc.), chopped

Camp Stove and At Home

In a large saucepan on your camp stove, heat 4 quarts of water to boiling. Add pasta and cook until crisp-tender, about 12 to 15 minutes. Pour off water and cool pasta. In a large salad bowl, add cooled pasta, salad dressing, Parmesan cheese and vegetables. Serves 6 to 8.

• A vinaigrette, such as Balsamic Vinaigrette (page 184), is also an excellent salad dressing choice.

POACHED TROUT SALAD

Dinner will reward the skill of your fishing partners. Otherwise, take the trout to the outdoors with you.

2 cups water or fish broth
1- to 1-1/2 pounds freshly caught trout, boned,
　　skinned and cut into fillets
2 heads of lettuce of your choice, rinsed and dried
2 ripe tomatoes, thinly sliced
1/2 cucumber, sliced
1 (15-ounce) can asparagus tips, drained (optional)
1 cup lemon dill dressing for fish (page 186)

Camp Stove and At Home

In a large frying pan, heat poaching liquids to boiling and add trout. Cook fish on low for 3 to 4 minutes on each side. Turn off heat and keep fish in the poaching liquids while finishing the salad.

Into a large salad bowl, tear lettuce into bite-sized pieces. Arrange tomatoes, cucumber and asparagus on the greens. Remove fillets from liquid and arrange on top. Serve with the dressing. Serves 6 to 8.

• Substitute fresh or canned salmon for the trout.

CHAPTER 10

Sandwiches

S andwiches are the fastest food for simple, sensational, outdoor meals. A variety of breads and a selection of fillings will satisfy hungry hikers and can be easily carried along the trail. Plastic self-sealing bags allow you to pack sliced meats, cheeses and other condiments at home. Store them in a refrigerator or cooler until lunchtime, and have each person prepare a delicious sandwich to their liking.

A shoebox is the perfect protection for sandwich bread because it has the same loaf shape and does not add weight to a backpack. Rolls and buns can be stored in lightweight shoeboxes as well. Special toothpaste-type squeeze tubes available at sporting goods stores can be filled with mustard, mayonnaise and even peanut butter and jelly.

Ready-to-Eat and Prepared Foods

Sandwiches are an essential part of outdoor eating. The number of convenience foods for your sandwich pantry is as unlimited as your imagination. Always include a variety of sandwich "fixings" and let guests mix and match. This chapter includes popular sandwich components and a few sandwich recipes.

Convenient condiments in tubes

Canned and fresh meats, fish, shellfish and poultry:

- Chicken
- Corned beef
- Crab
- Deviled ham
- Ham
- Kippered snacks
- Left-over cooked meats
- Mussels
- Oysters
- Pastrami
- Paté
- Range chicken
- Roast beef spread
- Salmon
- Sardines
- Shrimp
- Spam
- Tuna
- Turkey

Fully cooked meats from your grocery case may be purchased in sealed packages. Many include sauces with the meat such as Meat Loaf with Tomato Sauce or Pulled Pork with Barbecue Sauce.

Vegetables:

- Avocado
- Cucumber
- Green pepper
- Lettuce
- Olives
- Onion
- Red onion
- Tomato

Cheeses:

- American
- Brie
- Cheddar
- Cream
- Feta
- Fontina
- Monterey Jack
- Swiss

Condiments:

- Barbecue sauce
- Cracked pepper
- Hummus
- Ketchup
- Marinades
- Mayonnaise
- Mustards
- Salad dressings
- Salt
- Sour cream
- Tomato sauce

• For a satisfying but easy sandwich, slice prepared **meat loaf** and place on slices of bread spread with tomato sauce or ketchup. On another slice of bread spread mayonnaise and sliced onion (optional). Sandwich together and enjoy!

• Spread mayonnaise onto thinly sliced **red onion and sliced tomatoes.** Sprinkle lightly with sugar and place between slices of bread.

• For a hearty **barbecue sandwich,** fill a hoagie bun with heated fully cooked pulled pork and barbecue sauce.

• For a **chicken salad sandwich,** drain 1 (10-ounce) can of cooked chicken. Add chopped celery, onion or green onion, mayonnaise and salt and pepper to taste. Spread mixture on a fresh-baked roll or croissant from the bakery.

CORNED BEEF SANDWICHES

1 (15-ounce) can corned beef, shredded
1/3 cup mayonnaise
1/3 cup brown mustard
1 small onion, sliced
8 slices rye bread

In a small bowl, blend corned beef with mayonnaise and mustard and spread on bread slices. Top with an onion slice. Serves 4.

GRILLED HAM AND
BRIE SANDWICHES

Grilled ham enhances the flavor of melted Brie.

3 tablespoons butter, softened
2 tablespoons Dijon mustard
6 slices Italian bread
12 slices country ham
8 ounces Brie cheese

Grill and At Home

In a small bowl, blend butter and Dijon mustard, and spread on both sides of the bread. Place bread on hot grill. When browned, turn over and top each slice with 2 slices of ham and 1 1/2 ounces of cheese. Grill until cheese melts. Serve open-faced or slice in triangle shapes for an appetizer. Serves 6.

SAUSAGE, PEPPER
AND ONION SANDWICHES

1 tablespoon oil
1 medium onion, thinly sliced
4 green peppers, cut into strips
2 pounds cooked sausage, such as Polish kielbasa
1 French baguette or 6 sub rolls, sliced

Camp Stove and At Home

In a large skillet, heat oil and sauté onions and peppers until soft, about 15 to 20 minutes. Slice sausage into bite-sized pieces and cook, stirring occasionally, for 15 minutes, until warmed completely. Spoon sausage and vegetables onto a sliced baguette. Serve warm. Serves 6 to 8.

Grill

Cook uncut sausage on the hot grill on medium heat, turning occasionally to prevent burning. In a large skillet, heat oil and sauté peppers and onions until soft. When sausage is thoroughly heated, about 20 minutes, cut into bite-sized pieces. Spoon sausage and vegetables onto a sliced baguette. Serve warm. Serves 6 to 8.

Dutch Oven

Heat a 12-inch Dutch oven over 12 to 15 hot coals until very hot. Add oil and stir in onions and peppers. Sauté, stirring occasionally, for 15 to 20 minutes, or until vegetables are soft. Slice sausage into bite-sized pieces, add to vegetables and cook for 20 minutes. Spoon mixture onto a sliced baguette. Serve warm. Serves 6 to 8.

Dutch Oven Lid

Place the lid of a 12-inch Dutch oven upside down on a lid holder over 12 to 15 hot coals and heat until very hot. Add oil and stir in onions and peppers. Sauté, stirring occasionally, about 15 to 20 minutes, until vegetables are soft. Remove and set aside.

Grill uncut sausage on the same lid until evenly browned and hot throughout, turning occasionally, about 15 minutes. Slice into bite-sized pieces, add to vegetables and spoon mixture onto a sliced baguette. Serve warm. Serves 6 to 8.

PASTRAMI AND TOMATO SANDWICH

4 to 6 tomatoes, sliced
2 tablespoons olive oil
1/2 teaspoon salt
1/4 teaspoon pepper
2 tablespoons honey mustard
6 sourdough rolls
12 slices pastrami
6 slices Swiss cheese

Grill and At Home

Brush tomato slices with olive oil and place on hot grill to cook for 5 minutes, turning as needed. Sprinkle with salt and pepper. Spread mustard on sourdough roll and grill with tomatoes, pastrami and cheese. Serve warm. Serves 6.

BARBECUE BEEF SANDWICHES

1 pound ground beef
1/3 cup barbecue sauce
1/4 cup ketchup
1/3 cup beef broth
4 hamburger buns or French rolls
4 slices Cheddar cheese, optional

Camp Stove and At Home

In a large frying pan, sauté ground beef until browned. Pour off drippings and add barbecue sauce, ketchup and broth. Cook on high heat for 10 to 15 minutes, stirring well. Fill rolls with meat mixture and top with cheese. Serves 4.

Dutch Oven

Heat a 12-inch Dutch oven over 12 to 15 hot coals until hot. Sauté ground beef until browned. Pour off drippings and add barbecue sauce, ketchup and broth. Cook for 10 to 15 minutes, stirring well. Fill rolls with meat mixture and top with cheese. Serves 4.

GRILLED CHEESE SANDWICHES

Children never turn down a simple melted cheese sandwich.

2 tablespoons butter, softened
4 slices bread
4 slices cheese, your choice

Camp Stove and At Home

Butter one side of each slice of bread. Place 2 slices of cheese on unbuttered sides. Top with remaining bread, buttered side up. Heat a large frying pan until hot, and add sandwiches, buttered side down. Cook on low heat, turning over when golden brown. Serve when cheese is melted and bread is evenly browned. Serves 2.

Dutch Oven Lid

Place the lid of a 12-inch Dutch oven upside down on a lid holder over 12 to 15 hot coals and heat until very hot. Butter one side of each slice of bread. Place 2 slices of cheese on unbuttered sides. Top with remaining slice, buttered side up, and place on lid. Cook, turning over when golden brown. Serve when cheese is melted and bread is evenly browned. Serves 2.

• For a spicy combination, use jalapeño chili with Monterey Jack cheese.

VEGETABLE AND FETA SANDWICHES

1 tablespoon olive oil
2 tablespoons balsamic vinegar
4 sourdough rolls, halved
1 (12-ounce) jar roasted red peppers, drained
1 (4-ounce) jar mushrooms, drained and sliced
1/2 pound feta cheese, crumbled
1 teaspoon cracked pepper

Grill and At Home

In a small bowl, blend olive oil and vinegar and spread mixture on 8 roll halves; heat on hot grill next to peppers and mushrooms (see •). When heated, put peppers, mushrooms, cheese and cracked pepper on the hot rolls and cover with remaining halves. Cut in half and serve warm. Serves 4.

• If your grill has "ribs" too far apart for peppers and mushrooms, oil a piece of pierced foil and grill on the foil.

SMOKED TURKEY POCKETS

6 pita pockets, halved
1/2 cup mayonnaise
12 slices smoked turkey
2 avocados, peeled and sliced
3 tomatoes, sliced

Grill and At Home

On a hot grill, heat pita pockets until thoroughly warmed. Open pita pockets and spread mayonnaise inside on both sides. Insert turkey, avocado and tomatoes. Serves 6.

Fun Fast Sandwich Ideas

Banana Dog—Spread peanut butter and honey on a hot dog bun. Wrap in plastic and add to your pack. At lunchtime, peel banana and add to the hot dog bun for a nutritious treat.

Inside-Out Sandwich—Roll a slice of luncheon meat and a slice of cheese around a bread stick. Stick toothpicks through the top to hold meat and cheese.

French Toast Sandwich—Make French toast on your camping trip. Grill the French toast on both sides. Place cheese and ham slices between them. Wrap with paper napkin and enjoy.

CHAPTER 11

Hot Dogs
and Sausage

Hot dogs sound so simple—and they are; for that reason they're the perfect staple for any camping or outdoor cooking event. In spite of their simplicity, there are many ways to enhance the flavor and presentation of traditional hot dogs by using a little creativity in the preparation. Kids love **Monster Dogs** (page 139) or **Pigs in a Blanket** (page 140), which are so easy to prepare. For heartier eaters, **Polish Sausage Bake** (page 141) is a meal everyone can enjoy.

Sausages and hot dogs are often fully cooked, and thus are perfectly safe for the outdoors. Also, these items are already spiced and flavored and usually just need to be heated through before serving. Their shape makes them ideal for stick cooking, skewered with vegetables or combined in other foods of your choosing.

The hot dog is universal—a version exists in every country. It is also a staple for Scouts, hikers, children and campers. It can be eaten by itself, in a bun, in a buttered and toasted roll, inside cornbread on a stick (corn dogs), at home, in the street and at the movies, the ball game, and the beach.

The hot dog is made of different blends of meats: pork, beef, turkey, chicken and combinations thereof. A hot dog cooks quickly and is served with mustard, ketchup, chili sauce or chili, cheese, onion, pickle relish, sauerkraut or piccalilli. Buy them in all sizes from little smokies to foot-longs.

Ready-to-Eat and Prepared Foods

Very convenient, the fully cooked hot dog is individually wrapped and ready to heat. A wide variety of fully cooked sausages includes the brown-and-serve variety. Condiments come in squeeze bottles, jars and easy-open cans for a super quick meal.

From a squeeze bottle or jar:

- Barbecue sauce
- Cajun sauce
- Cheese spread
- Ketchup
- Mayonnaise
- Mustard
- Pickles
- Relish
- Salsa
- Sour cream

From a can:

- Chili
- Chili sauce
- Hot peppers
- Sauerkraut

Types of American hot dogs:

There are many types: beef, pork, turkey, chicken, meatless (soy) or mixed. Some have a natural casing and others have no casing at all. Varieties include Chicago, kosher, cheese-filled, regular size and foot-long, and short, fat and mini-hot dogs.

WHISTLE DOG

Garnish with Cheddar cheese and bacon.

CONEY ISLAND DOG

Garnish with Cheddar cheese, chili sauce and hot peppers.

TEX-MEX DOG

Garnish with melted Monterey Jack cheese, salsa and sour cream.

BARBECUE DOG

Garnish with barbecue sauce and bacon.

YODEL DOG

Garnish with Swiss cheese and mustard.

CAJUN DOG

Garnish with Cajun sauce, salsa and Monterey Jack cheese.

BEANS AND WIENERS

Easy and good enough for President and Mrs. Reagan (photo page 5). This recipe could be a child's first cooking lesson.

1 package hot dogs, as needed, sliced into fourths
2 (15.5-ounce) cans pork and beans

Camp Stove and At Home

In a large skillet, combine hot dogs and beans. Heat on medium low until hot and bubbly. Serves 4 to 6.

• To take on a hike, pour cooked pork and beans and a hot dog tied with a long piece of dental floss into wide-mouth thermos. In a bun, add the pork and beans with the hot dog. After you eat, you have a piece of dental floss to clean your teeth.

DOG BISCUITS

8 hot dogs
1 (7.5-ounce) package refrigerated biscuits (8 count)

Grill and At home

Thread hot dogs on skewers and roast over a bed of hot coals for 5 minutes, turning often to cook evenly.

Squeeze each biscuit between your palms to create a flat square. Using one biscuit per hot dog, carefully surround heated hot dog completely with the dough. Pinch dough tightly closed at each end and along the sides. (Heat from the roasted hot dog helps to cook the inside of the biscuit.) Roast over a bed of hot coals, turning slowly to cook dough completely through. When evenly browned, about 5 to 10 minutes, serve with mustard and ketchup, as desired. Serves 4.

ITALIAN SAUSAGE IN TOMATO SAUCE

2 pounds Italian sausage (mild or hot), casing removed
1 (28-ounce) jar spaghetti sauce
Cooked pasta or focaccia bread, as desired

Camp Stove and At Home

In a large frying pan, cook sausage, stirring until crumbled and thoroughly cooked. Pour off drippings; add spaghetti sauce. Cook, stirring occasionally, until heated thoroughly, about 10 minutes. Serve on cooked pasta or as a dip for focaccia bread. Serves 6 to 8.

Dutch Oven

Heat a 12-inch Dutch oven over 12 hot coals. Cook sausage, stirring, until crumbled and thoroughly cooked. Pour off drippings; add spaghetti sauce. Cook, stirring occasionally, until heated thoroughly, about 10 minutes. Serve on cooked pasta or as a dip for focaccia bread. Serves 6 to 8.

• Cooked mushrooms, onions or peppers may be added to the sauce.

MONSTER DOGS

8 hot dogs
8 hot dog buns, grilled
Condiments of your choice

Cut slits in hot dogs two-thirds of the way through to create "arms" and "legs."

Camp Stove and At Home

In a large skillet, add hot dogs and cook until evenly browned on all sides. (When cooking, the "limbs" will curl, creating a "monster dog.") Place on grilled buns and serve with your favorite condiments. Serves 4.

Grill

On a hot grill, add hot dogs and cook until evenly browned on all sides. (When cooking, the "limbs" will curl, creating a "monster dog.") Place on grilled buns and serve with your favorite condiments. Serves 4.

Ooh . . . scary . . . monster dogs

DOG-GONE-ITS

And that's what you'll say when these are all gone.

8 hot dogs, cut into bite-sized chunks
16 cherry tomatoes
1 (5-ounce) jar cocktail onions
Bamboo skewers

Grill and At Home

Thread meat, tomatoes and onions alternately onto skewers. Cook 4 inches from a bed of hot coals for 5 to 7 minutes, turning often. Serves 4.

PIGS IN A BLANKET

1 package hot dogs, cut in half
1 (8-ounce) package refrigerated crescent rolls

Unroll dough and squeeze seams together to make one big rectangle. Divide evenly into 16 small squares. Wrap each square around a hot dog half.

Dutch Oven

Preheat a 12-inch Dutch oven over 9 hot coals for 5 minutes. Set 3 canning jar rings or flat rocks in the oven bottom. Place wrapped hot dogs into an oiled round cake pan and set it on the rings. Cover with Dutch oven lid and place 15 hot coals on top. Bake, covered, for 20 minutes, or until rolls are evenly browned. Serves 4.

POLISH SAUSAGE BAKE

1 tablespoon oil

6 boiling onions, peeled and cut in half

2 pounds Polish sausage, cut into 2-inch chunks

2 stalks celery, cut into 2-inch pieces

4 potatoes, peeled and quartered

4 carrots, peeled and cut into chunks

1/2 head of cabbage, cut into 2 or 3 wedges

1 cup chicken or vegetable broth

1/2 teaspoon salt

1/4 teaspoon pepper

Camp Stove and At Home

In a large skillet, heat oil. Add onions and sausage and cook for 10 minutes, stirring until sausage has browned. Add celery, potatoes, carrots and cabbage, stirring well. Cook, covered, for 30 to 40 minutes on medium-low heat, until vegetables are tender, adding a little broth as needed to keep food moist. Salt and pepper and serve. Serves 4 to 6.

Dutch Oven

Heat a 12-inch Dutch oven over 12 to 15 hot coals and heat oil. Add onions and sausage and cook for 10 minutes, stirring until sausage has browned. Add celery, potatoes, carrots and cabbage, stirring well. Cook, covered, for 30 to 40 minutes, until vegetables are tender, adding a little broth as needed to keep food moist. Salt and pepper and serve. Serves 4 to 6.

BACON DOGS 'N TOTS

Bacon, as needed
Hot dogs, as desired
Tater Tots, as desired (thawed)
Toothpicks

Grill and At Home

Cut bacon strips and hot dogs into thirds. Wrap the hot dog sections and the Tater Tots with cut strips of bacon, securing each piece with a toothpick. Grill over hot coals, turning occasionally, to cook evenly. When bacon is evenly crisp, remove from grill and serve as an appetizer or snack.

No one can eat just one of these appetizers

CHAPTER 12

Main Dishes

I t's easier than most people realize to produce elegant and impressive main dish meals outdoors. Whether you use a camp stove, Dutch oven or other means of cooking, main dish recipes take on a splendid, unique flavor when prepared outdoors. I have adapted several of my family favorites for outdoor cooking. Two of my most-requested dishes are **Pistol Rock Chicken** and hearty **Enchilada Pie** (pages 145 and 149). You too can experiment with your own family favorites by using some of these outdoor cooking tips.

Once you're comfortable with the basics of Dutch oven, camp stove, aluminum foil or grill cooking, you'll be amazed at the creative ways you can prepare your favorite recipes outdoors. You'll have the same success you've known at home on your own oven or rangetop.

Ready-to-Eat and Prepared Foods

When using traditional methods, you know all too well that main dishes need time to fix. Delicious baked meals can start with fully cooked meats prepared in a fraction of the time.

In the meat case or the frozen food case are such items as fully cooked, always tender beef, pork and chicken combined with numerous seasonings. Selections change daily and from market to market. Don't forget to shop the deli departments for ready-to-heat-and-eat ideas as well.

SWEET AND SOUR PORK

2 tablespoons oil
1 medium onion, chopped
1 green pepper, chopped
1 (1-pound) fully cooked pork roast, cut into 1-inch cubes
1/2 cup sweet and sour sauce
1 (10-ounce) package frozen pea pods
1 (15-ounce) can pineapple tidbits, drained
Cooked rice, about 4 cups

Camp Stove and At Home

In a large skillet, heat oil and sauté onion and green pepper until soft. Add pork and sweet and sour sauce and cook until boiling. Stir in frozen pea pods and pineapple and cook until hot. Serve over cooked rice. Serves 4.

BAKED HAM AND VEGETABLE DINNER

3 tablespoons butter or margarine
2 fully cooked thick ham slices (1/2- to 1-inch thick)
1 (15-ounce) can yams in syrup
1 (12-ounce) package frozen squash (cubed)

Grill and At Home

In a large skillet, melt butter or margarine. Add ham and brown for 2 to 3 minutes on each side. Add yams and frozen squash. Cook, covered, 15 to 20 minutes, until heated through and syrup is reduced. Serves 4.

PISTOL ROCK CHICKEN

1 whole chicken, skinned and cut into pieces
1/2 teaspoon salt
1/4 teaspoon pepper
1/8 teaspoon garlic salt
1 cup all-purpose flour
2 tablespoons oil
1 (15-ounce) can crushed tomatoes
1 (8-ounce) can sliced mushrooms, drained

Rinse chicken thoroughly and pat dry with paper towels. In a 1-gallon plastic self-sealing bag, add salt, pepper, garlic salt and flour. Add chicken, close the bag and shake well to coat.

Camp Stove and At Home

In a large skillet, heat oil and brown chicken well on all sides. Pour off excess oil and add tomato sauce and mushrooms. Simmer, covered, stirring occasionally, for 1 hour. Remove cover and cook 15 minutes, until sauce thickens, stirring frequently. Serves 4.

Dutch Oven

Place a 12-inch Dutch oven over 12 to 15 hot coals. Add oil to hot Dutch oven and brown chicken well on all sides. Pour off excess oil and add tomato sauce and mushrooms. Simmer, covered, stirring occasionally, for 1 hour. Remove cover and cook 15 minutes, until sauce thickens, stirring frequently. Serves 4.

CHICKEN SOUPER

1 (11.5-ounce) can cream of mushroom soup
1 (11.5-ounce) can cream of celery soup
1 (11.5-ounce) can cream of chicken soup
2 soup cans water
2 cups white rice, uncooked
1 (3-pound) chicken, skinned and cut up
1/2 (1.3-ounce) package dried onion soup mix

Dutch Oven

Heat a 12-inch Dutch oven over 12 to 15 hot coals. Blend soups (undiluted), water and rice in Dutch oven. Arrange chicken pieces on top; sprinkle with dry soup mix. Cook, covered, for 45 to 60 minutes, until chicken is cooked and rice has absorbed liquid. Let it rest, covered, 10 minutes before serving. Serves 4 to 6.

At Home

Follow the above **Dutch oven** directions, using a roasting pan at 350°F. Cook, covered, 45 to 60 minutes. Serves 4 to 6.

CORNISH GAME HENS IN SAUCE

2 tablespoons olive oil
2 Cornish game hens
2 large onions, cut in half
1 cup chicken broth
1/2 cup white wine, or 1/4 cup cider vinegar or
        juice of 1 lemon
4 cloves garlic, crushed

Camp Stove and At Home

In a large skillet, heat oil. Brown game hens evenly. Add onions and cook 5 minutes to soften. Add broth, wine and garlic. Simmer, covered, for 1 to 1 1/2 hours, or until hens are very tender (legs and wings should "wiggle" easily). Serves 2.

Dutch Oven

Heat a 12-inch Dutch oven over 12 to 15 hot coals. Heat oil and brown game hens evenly. Add onions and cook 5 minutes to soften. Add broth, wine and garlic. Simmer, covered, for 1 to 1 1/2 hours, until hens are very tender (legs and wings should "wiggle" easily). Serves 2.

• Whole chicken, duck, goose or rabbit can be substituted for the game hens.

BARBECUE COUNTRY-STYLE PORK RIBS

Country-style ribs are meatier than a full rack.

  2 tablespoons oil
  3 pounds boneless country-style ribs
  Salt
  Pepper
  12 boiling onions
  2 cups beef broth
  1 recipe mild barbecue sauce (page 179)

Dutch Oven

In a 12-inch Dutch oven over 9 hot coals, heat oil and brown ribs seasoned with salt and pepper on both sides. Add whole onions and cook until browned. Add broth, cover and place 15 hot coals on top. Cook for 45 minutes to 1 hour, until meat is tender. Pour barbecue sauce onto meat and cook, covered, for 30 minutes. Serves 4 to 6.

At Home

Preheat the oven to 350°F. In a skillet, brown meat in oil. Add whole onions and cook until browned. Place meat and broth in a roasting pan. Cook, covered with aluminum foil, 45 minutes; pour barbecue sauce onto meat and cook for 30 minutes. Serves 4 to 6.

• Any prepared barbecue sauce can be substituted in this recipe.

MARINATED LOIN OF PORK

1 recipe marinade for pork (page 183)
1 3-pound loin of pork
2 tablespoons olive oil
2 tablespoons butter or margarine
2 cups chicken broth
3 tablespoons beurre manie (page 176)
1/4 teaspoon salt
1/8 teaspoon pepper

In a 1-gallon plastic self-sealing bag, add meat and marinade. Place in a refrigerator or cooler overnight.

Camp Stove and At Home

Remove loin from marinade and pat dry. In a large frying pan, heat oil and butter or margarine and brown loin on all sides. Cook for 30 minutes, turning occasionally, and set aside.

In a saucepan, boil leftover marinade 5 minutes and add broth. Simmer, covered, for 60 minutes. Remove loin and add broth to large pan. On high heat stir in beurre manie and whisk to thicken liquids in the pan. Salt and pepper as desired. Slice meat thinly, reheat briefly and serve with sauce. Serves 6 to 8.

Dutch Oven and Camp Stove

Remove loin from marinade and pat dry. Heat a 12-inch Dutch oven over 12 to 15 hot coals. Brown meat in oil and butter or margarine on all sides. Cook 30 minutes, turning occasionally and set aside. In a saucepan, boil leftover marinade 5 minutes and add broth. Simmer, covered, for 60 minutes. Remove loin and add broth to the Dutch oven. Add beurre manie and whisk to thicken liquids. Salt and pepper as desired. Slice meat thinly, reheat briefly and serve with sauce. Serves 6 to 8.

• *Beurre manie* is a paste of butter and flour thinned with liquid as you would for making gravy. The premade butter makes a pan-reduction sauce easier and without concern for lumps. At the end of the recipe, heat the liquid on high heat and whisk the *Beurre manie* into the liquid, stirring rapidly to smooth the sauce. The liquids are reduced at the same time by evaporation. Gravy should be this easy to make.

ENCHILADA PIE

2 pounds lean ground beef
1 medium onion, chopped
1 (11.5-ounce) can condensed tomato soup
2 (10-ounce) cans mild or hot enchilada sauce
1 cup water
9 (8-inch) flour or corn tortillas
1 1/2 to 2 cups (8 ounces) Cheddar or
    Monterey Jack cheese, shredded

Dutch Oven

Heat a 12-inch Dutch oven over 9 hot coals. Brown meat and onion. Pour off drippings. Add soup, enchilada sauce and water and simmer 5 minutes. Spoon 2/3 of this mixture into a medium bowl, leaving remaining 1/3 in the Dutch oven. Arrange 2 to 3 tortillas over the meat mixture and sprinkle with 1/3 of the cheese. Layer with half of the remaining meat mixture and 1/3 of the cheese; repeat. Cover with Dutch oven lid and place 12 to 15 hot coals on top. Cook, covered, 10 to 15 minutes, or until cheese melts and tortillas soften. Serves 6 to 8.

At Home

Preheat oven to 350°F. In a large skillet, brown meat with onion. Pour off drippings. Add soup, enchilada sauce and water, and simmer 5 minutes.

In a 9 x 13-inch dish, layer 1/3 of the meat mixture, then 2 or 3 tortillas, and 1/3 of the cheese; repeat with remaining ingredients. Cook, covered, 10 to 15 minutes, or until cheese melts and tortillas soften. Serves 6 to 8.

Hearty, delicious enchilada pie

CHICKEN AND SALSA OLÉ

1/2 cup all-purpose flour
1/2 teaspoon salt
1/2 teaspoon chili powder
1/2 teaspoon garlic powder
6 to 8 chicken breasts, boned and skinned
2 tablespoons oil
2 (7-ounce) cans chili peppers
2 cups Cheddar cheese, shredded
1 (14- to 20-ounce) jar salsa

In a 1-gallon plastic self-sealing bag, mix flour, salt, chili powder, and garlic powder; shake the chicken in the bag.

Camp Stove and At Home

In a large skillet, heat oil and add chicken pieces. Cook on each side for 10 minutes. Split chili peppers open and place one on top of each chicken breast. Sprinkle each with 1/2 cup cheese. Pour salsa around the chicken and cook, covered, for 5 to 10 minutes, until heated thoroughly and cheese is melted. Serve with tortillas and refried beans or Spanish rice (page 170). Serves 6 to 8.

Dutch Oven

Heat a 12-inch Dutch oven over 12 to 15 hot coals. Heat oil and add chicken pieces. Cook on each side for 10 minutes. Split chili peppers open and place one on top of each chicken breast. Sprinkle each with 1/2 cup cheese. Pour salsa around the chicken and cook, covered, for 5 minutes, until heated thoroughly and cheese is melted. Serve with tortillas and refried beans or Spanish rice (page 170). Serves 6 to 8.

BEEF STEW

1/2 cup all-purpose flour

1 teaspoon salt

1/2 teaspoon pepper

3 pounds beef stew meat or chuck roast, cut into 3/4-
inch cubes

2 tablespoons oil

2 onions, diced

1 chili (as desired for spice), diced

3 fresh tomatoes, peeled and crushed, or 1
(14.5-ounce) can whole, peeled tomatoes (see •)

6 to 8 cloves of garlic, whole, unpeeled

6 cups beef broth

6 potatoes, peeled and quartered

8 carrots, peeled and sliced

• Always wear rubber gloves or wash your hands thoroughly when handling *chili*. Avoid rubbing your eyes. Small chilies are more pungent (concentrated) than larger, milder ones.

• Tomatoes can be easily peeled by *blanching* in boiling water briefly and then plunging into ice water.

Camp Stove and At Home

On a sheet of wax paper or in a 1-gallon plastic self-sealing bag, combine flour, salt and pepper and dredge meat evenly. In a large skillet, heat oil and brown meat on all sides. Remove meat from pan and set aside.

Add onions and chili; cook until soft. Add tomatoes and garlic, and cook, stirring frequently, for 10 minutes. Add browned meat and broth. Cook, covered, 2 to 3 hours, or until meat is tender. Add potatoes and carrots and cook for 45 minutes more, or until potatoes and carrots are tender. Serves 6 to 8.

Dutch Oven

Stews take several hours to cook in a Dutch oven. If you will be available to add ingredients and tend the fire, stew recipes are worth the wait.

CAMP CHILI

1 pound ground beef
1 medium onion, diced
1 (15-ounce) can kidney beans or red beans
1 (11.5-ounce) can cream of tomato soup
2 tablespoons chili powder
1/2 teaspoon salt
1/4 teaspoon pepper

Camp Stove and At Home

In a large skillet, brown ground beef and onion. Pour off drippings and add kidney beans, soup, chili powder, salt and pepper. Simmer, covered, until very hot, about 10 to 15 minutes. Serves 6 to 8.

Dutch Oven

Heat a 12-inch Dutch oven over 12 to 15 hot coals. Brown ground beef and onion. Pour off drippings and add kidney beans, soup, chili powder, salt and pepper. Simmer, covered, for 15 to 20 minutes. Serves 6 to 8.

• A package of chili seasonings can be substituted for chili powder.

SLOPPY JOE BISCUIT BAKE

1 medium onion, chopped
2 pounds lean ground beef
2 (1.3-ounce) packages Sloppy Joe seasoning mix
2 (6-ounce) cans tomato paste
2 cups water
1 (16-ounce) package prepared refrigerator biscuits

Dutch Oven

Heat a 12-inch Dutch oven over 9 hot coals. Brown onion and ground beef. Add seasoning mix, tomato paste and water, stirring well, and bring to a boil. Separate individual biscuits and place on top of the meat mixture. Cover with Dutch oven lid and place 15 hot coals on top. Cook, covered, for 15 to 20 minutes, or until biscuits are browned and cooked through. Serves 4 to 6.

At Home

Preheat the oven to 350°F. In a large skillet, brown onion and ground beef; pour off drippings and add seasoning mix, tomato paste and water, stirring well; bring to a boil. Transfer mixture to an oven-safe dish. Separate individual biscuits and place on top of the meat mixture. Bake 15 minutes, until biscuits are browned and cooked through. Serves 4 to 6.

• Canned Sloppy Joe mix can be used in place of the packaged seasoning.

• If the handle of your skillet is oven-safe, you don't need to transfer the mixture to an oven-safe dish.

TURKEY AND PROSCIUTTO CUTLETS

1 tablespoon butter or margarine
1 tablespoon oil
1/4 cup all-purpose flour
1/2 teaspoon salt
1/4 teaspoon pepper
8 turkey breast cutlets, 1/3-inch thick
4 slices prosciutto ham
4 slices Fontina cheese
1 lemon
1 cup chicken broth
1/2 cup heavy cream or milk

Camp Stove and At Home

In a large frying pan, heat butter or margarine and oil. On a piece of wax paper combine flour, salt and pepper. Place 4 cutlets on a clean surface; place 1 slice of ham and 1 slice of cheese on each cutlet. Top with remaining cutlets. Dredge the stuffed cutlets in the flour mixture and fry on both sides until a golden color. Remove from the pan and set aside.

Add the juice of 1 lemon, chicken broth and cream to the pan drippings. Cook on high heat, stirring rapidly, until sauce reduces and thickens. Pour the sauce on the cutlets and serve. Serves 4.

STUFFED SHRIMP IN GARLIC AND HERB BUTTER

A company recipe that looks far more complicated than it is. And the flavor and presentation are worth every step.

2 pounds jumbo shrimp, peeled and deveined
1 recipe mushroom stuffing (page 172)
1 recipe garlic and herb butter or margarine (page 177)
1 lemon

Split shrimp halfway through the flesh (where vein was removed) from head to tail. Spread stuffing into the cavity.

Camp Stove and At Home

In a large skillet, melt half of the herbed butter or margarine. Add shrimp and stir until well coated. Cook, covered, 4 to 5 minutes, or until shrimp is opaque and pink throughout. Remove shrimp from the pan and set aside.

In the skillet on high heat, add remaining herb butter and juice of 1 lemon; stir into pan drippings until smooth. Cook, stirring rapidly, until sauce reduces and thickens. Serve the sauce with the shrimp. Serves 6.

Dutch Oven

Heat a 12-inch Dutch oven over 12 to 15 hot coals. Melt half of the herbed butter or margarine. Add shrimp and stir until well coated. Cook, covered, 8 to 10 minutes or until shrimp is opaque and pink throughout. Remove from Dutch oven and set aside.

In the Dutch oven, add remaining herb butter and juice of 1 lemon; stir into pan drippings until smooth. Cook, stirring rapidly, until sauce reduces and thickens. Serve the sauce with shrimp. Serves 6.

• A commercial stuffing mix can be used, if desired.

CHAPTER 13

One-Dish Meals

Hearty and satisfying one-dish meals are a boon to any outdoor excursion. Whether you're on the trail or around a campfire, you'll find that these simple yet satisfying recipes were designed for quick preparation using readily available ingredients. In addition to traditional stews and poultry dishes, try innovative recipes like **Goat Cheese and Caramelized Onion Pizzelle** (page 158). It's yummy!

A single pot makes cooking a breeze and cleanup even easier. And these one-dish dinners can be adapted to fit any size pot you have. I've even used small, individual-size Dutch ovens for dishes that children in particular love to prepare and eat. Or, you may want to prepare large quantities of the one-dish favorites just to have planned leftovers for another meal.

Ready-to-Eat and Prepared Foods

It's fun to invent any number of new one-dish meals by having a variety of groceries in your camping pantry. Three essential categories of foods are potatoes, rice and pasta which can be combined with sauces, vegetables and/or meats to make a savory meal.

Potatoes—from the refrigerated case:
- Hash browns
- Sliced

Potatoes—from the freezer case:
- Baked
- Hash browns
- Home fries
- Mashed
- Twice baked

From the shelf:
- Au gratin
- Twice baked

Rice:
- Brown
- Instant
- Rice dishes
- Risotto
- Spanish
- Uncle Ben's
- Wild

Other:
- Frozen macaroni and cheese
- Frozen ravioli, lasagna
- Packaged macaroni and cheese

Meats, poultry and seafood:
- Chicken
- Fish sticks
- Ground beef
- Sausage

Fully cooked meats:
Very convenient with their own sauce, these are found in the meat or deli case in the supermarket. Heat, add vegetables and a carbohydrate, and serve. The frozen food case also has many prepared meats from which to choose.

BARBECUE SKILLET

In a medium skillet, heat 1 (17-ounce) package fully cooked shredded beef with barbecue sauce and serve on a bun. An excellent accompaniment is twice-baked potatoes. Serves 4.

FAST SLOPPY JOES

In a medium skillet, brown 1 pound ground beef; pour off drippings and add 1 (16-ounce) can Sloppy Joe sauce. Serve on fresh bakery rolls. Serves 4.

RAVIOLI DINNER

In a large saucepan, heat 1 (28-ounce) jar of spaghetti sauce. Add 1 (25-ounce) package frozen, fully cooked ravioli. Heat thoroughly and top with Parmesan cheese. Serves 4.

BARBECUE BEEF AND BISCUIT BAKE

3 pounds coarsely ground beef (chili meat)
1 cup barbecue sauce
1 cup ketchup
1/2 teaspoon onion powder
1/2 teaspoon garlic powder
1 cup beef broth
2 cups sharp Cheddar cheese, shredded
1 (7.5-ounce) package buttermilk biscuits (10 biscuits)

Dutch Oven

Heat a 12-inch Dutch oven over 9 hot coals. Brown the ground beef. Pour off drippings and add barbecue sauce, ketchup, onion powder, garlic powder and beef broth. Cook 10 minutes, until steaming. Sprinkle cheese on top and arrange biscuits on top of the cheese. Cover with Dutch oven lid and place 15 hot coals on top. Cook, covered, for 20 minutes, or until biscuits are golden brown and cooked through. Serves 8.

At Home

Follow the above **Dutch oven** directions using a baking dish in your oven. Bake at 350°F. for 15 minutes, or until biscuits are golden brown.

GOAT CHEESE AND CARAMELIZED
ONION PIZZELLE

An absolutely delicious treat as an appetizer or main dish. You'll want to make this often.

Pizzelle crust, 1/4 recipe (page 194)
2 tablespoons olive oil
2 medium onions, thinly sliced
Salt
Pepper
2 tomatoes, thinly sliced (see •)
8 ounces feta cheese, crumbled

• *Sun-dried tomatoes* will add even more flavor and can be substituted for fresh.

Dutch Oven

Prepare 1/4 pizzelle crust recipe. Heat a 12-inch Dutch oven over 9 hot coals. Stretch and spread 1/4 crust dough on a 10-inch cake pan and brush it with 1 tablespoon olive oil.

In the hot Dutch oven, sauté onions in 1 tablespoon olive oil until browned and caramelized, about 20 minutes. Salt and pepper, as desired. Pour off any liquid from the onions and arrange evenly on the crust. Top with tomatoes and goat cheese. Place cake pan on 3 canning jar rings or Dutch oven rack inside the Dutch oven. Cover with Dutch oven lid and place 15 hot coals on top. Bake, covered, until crust is cooked and cheese is melted, about 1 hour. Let it rest, covered, 10 minutes before serving. Serves 4.

At Home

Prepare 1/4 pizzelle crust recipe. Stretch and spread it on a 10-inch cake pan and brush it with 1 tablespoon olive oil. In a large skillet in 1 tablespoon of olive oil, sauté the onions until browned and caramelized, about 20 minutes. Pour off any liquid from the onions and arrange evenly on the dough. Salt and pepper, as desired. Top with tomatoes and goat cheese. Bake at 375°F. for 30 minutes. Let it rest 10 minutes before serving. Serves 4.

LAYERED FISH STEW

Guida, a dear friend from the Azores, Portugal, shared this family favorite. It will be a favorite of yours too.

- 2 tablespoons olive oil
- 1 medium onion, thinly sliced
- 4 garlic cloves, minced
- 6 fresh tomatoes, sliced
- 2 potatoes, peeled and thinly sliced
- 1 1/2 to 2 pounds of any firm white fish fillets (such as cod)
- 2 zucchini, sliced
- 1 teaspoon salt
- 1/2 teaspoon pepper
- 1/2 cup water

Camp Stove and At Home

In a large pot with lid, heat olive oil. Layer 1/2 of the onion, garlic, tomatoes, potatoes, fish, zucchini, salt, pepper and water. Repeat in the same order with remaining ingredients. Simmer, covered, for 1 hour. Serves 6 to 8.

Dutch Oven

Heat a 12-inch Dutch oven over 9 hot coals; add olive oil. Layer 1/2 of the onion, garlic, tomatoes, potatoes, fish, zucchini, salt, pepper and water. Repeat in the same order with remaining ingredients. Cover with Dutch oven lid and place 15 hot coals on top. Simmer, covered, for 1 hour. Serves 6 to 8.

ORIENTAL NOODLE STIR FRY

3 (3-ounce) packages oriental noodles
3 tablespoons oil
1 red pepper, sliced
2 (6-ounce) cans shrimp, drained
1 (7-ounce) can asparagus tips, drained
1 (7-ounce) can mushrooms, drained
1/4 cup lite soy sauce

Camp Stove and At Home

Cook noodles following package directions. Pour off water and set aside.

In a large skillet, heat oil and sauté red pepper. Add cooked noodles, shrimp, asparagus, mushrooms and soy sauce. Stir fry for 10 minutes, or until ingredients are hot. Serves 4 to 6.

ORZO AND CHICKEN DINNER

3 tablespoons butter or margarine
2 (10-ounce) cans chicken, drained
1 (4.5-ounce) can sliced mushrooms, drained
3 cups chicken broth
1 (10-ounce) package frozen peas
1 cup orzo (tiny rice-shaped pasta)

Camp Stove and At Home

In a large frying pan, melt butter or margarine. Add chicken and mushrooms and sauté for 2 minutes. Add broth, peas and orzo. Cook, covered, on low heat for 20 to 25 minutes, or until all liquids are absorbed. Serves 4 to 6.

Dutch Oven

Heat a 12-inch Dutch oven over 12 hot coals. Melt the butter or margarine and add chicken and mushrooms. Cook for 2 minutes. Add broth, peas and orzo. Cook, covered, for 20 to 25 minutes, or until all liquids are absorbed. Serves 4 to 6.

POLENTA AND SEAFOOD

2 tablespoons butter or margarine
1 pound prepared polenta in a tube (or recipe below)
1 pound shrimp, crab, fish or any choice of seafood
1 (28-ounce) jar marinara sauce

Camp Stove and At Home

In a large skillet, melt butter or margarine. Add polenta cut in 1/2-inch slices or wedges, and brown on both sides. Add seafood and pour marinara over seafood. Simmer, covered, for 5 minutes, or until sauce is hot. Serves 4 to 6.

Dutch Oven

Heat a 12-inch Dutch oven over 12 hot coals. Melt butter or margarine; add polenta slices or wedges, and brown on both sides. Add seafood and pour marinara over seafood. Cook, covered, for 10 minutes, or until sauce is hot. Serves 4 to 6.

• Fresh, frozen or canned seafood may be used.

POLENTA

An Italian staple, *polenta* is made from cornmeal, similar to Cream of Wheat, cooked and then refrigerated to firm. Serve at breakfast with syrup or as a side dish.

3 cups water
1 teaspoon salt
2 tablespoons butter or margarine
3/4 cup yellow cornmeal
3/4 cup fresh Parmesan cheese, shredded

In a medium saucepan, combine water, salt and butter or margarine, and heat until boiling. Add cornmeal gradually, stirring or whisking to avoid lumps. Simmer, stirring often, until thick, about 10 to 15 minutes. Remove from heat and stir in Parmesan cheese. Line the bottom of a 9-inch pie plate with plastic wrap and add polenta. Smooth the surface with a table knife. Chill, covered with plastic wrap, at least 1 hour. When firm, cut into slices or wedges and serve with butter or margarine. The slices or wedges can also be brushed with olive oil and grilled over hot coals. Serves 4 to 6.

RISOTTO AND SALMON DINNER

Risotto is a blend of Arborio rice sautéed in butter or margarine and cooked with broth, added one-half cup at a time, and repeated until all liquid is absorbed. It is labor intensive unless cooked ahead in a microwave oven. Chill and take it with you.

> **2 (5-ounce) packages risotto**
> **2 (6-ounce) cans salmon**
> **1 (28-ounce) jar Alfredo sauce (or 1 1/2 Alfredo**
>   **sauce recipes below)**
> **1/2 cup green onions, chopped**
> **1/2 cup Parmesan cheese, shredded**

Camp Stove and At Home

Prepare risotto following package directions. Set aside.

In a large saucepan, combine salmon, Alfredo sauce and green onions. Cook 10 minutes to heat all ingredients thoroughly. Spoon salmon sauce over risotto and sprinkle with cheese. Serves 4 to 6.

• **Alfredo sauce** is made by melting 3 tablespoons butter and stirring in 3 tablespoons flour (or 3 tablespoons of beurre manie, page 176) until smooth. Cook for 1 minute. Add 2 cups of heavy cream, salt and pepper and cook, stirring constantly, until sauce thickens. This is a mellow but tasty sauce to serve with pasta and vegetables.

CHAPTER 14

Side Dishes

W hen you are cooking out of doors, there's no need to omit the traditional courses that add variety and nutrition to meals. Vegetables, potatoes, rice, and pasta are perfect accompaniments to grilled meat, poultry or seafood. And most of these wonderful side dishes can be prepared just as easily outdoors as at home.

When outdoors, you'll want to pay close attention to healthy, nutritional meals and snacks. Vitamins found in vegetables, proteins from grains and legumes, and energy from carbohydrates are essential for hiking, camping and other activities. Vegetables can be cleaned, prepared and placed in plastic self-sealing storage bags at home. Kept in a refrigerator or cooler, they remain fresh until ready to eat or cook. **Provencale Tomatoes** and **Cowboy Potatoes** (pages 174 and 166) give new life to everyday vegetables.

Ready-to-Eat and Prepared Foods

A side dish enhances a very plain, simple main course and can be comfortingly familiar as well as new and exciting. The frozen foods section in your supermarket provides many ready-to-heat side dishes. There are also many packaged on-the-shelf side dishes that require only the addition of water and perhaps butter or margarine or other fresh ingredients.

Vegetables:

Frozen vegetables such as corn, broccoli, cauliflower, and a host of others are now available with sauce included. Canned vegetables, however, are more practical for easy storing and toting outdoors.

Potatoes:

In the *freezer section* you will find multiple varieties and brands of potatoes:

- French fries
- Fries and onion ringers
- Hash browns
- Tater Tots
- Toaster hash browns
- Topped baked potatoes
- Twice-baked potatoes
- Whipped potatoes

On the shelf is a variety of *dehydrated* potatoes:

- Mashed potatoes
- Potato skillet meals
- Potatoes au gratin
- Scalloped potatoes

Rice:

Flavored rice pouches are available. A great many brands and flavors include pilafs, couscous, tabbouleh, and creative grains such as brown rice and pearl. Many of these side dishes require adding water, oil, butter or margarine and cooking on low heat in a covered pan.

Stuffing:

Stuffing adds a home-cooked touch to a poultry dinner. The mixes come in a variety of brands, packages, and flavors, including chicken, pork, beef and cornbread, plus savory and holiday flavors.

Pasta:

How did we live without the huge variety of pasta we enjoy today? Pasta dishes have become as plentiful in America as in Italy.

Frozen pasta varieties include:

- Fettuccini Alfredo
- Macaroni and cheese
- Pasta with sauce
- Ready-to-bake lasagna
- Spaghetti with meat sauce
- Three-cheese ravioli

Pasta on-the-shelf varieties include:

- Broccoli and Carrots in Creamy Cheddar Sauce
- Creamy Cheddar Pasta
- Macaroni and cheese
- Pasta with vegetables and sauce

Pasta from the pantry:

Many companies offer easy-to-cook pasta and sauces in a variety of flavors; for example: Fettuccini with Classic Alfredo Sauce and everyone's favorite, Macaroni and Cheese. They are available in boxes and in soft envelopes.

About Pasta—

History claims that Marco Polo brought the idea for noodles to Italy from China. The truth is this food existed in both places independently before Marco Polo's trips. Almost every country has a form of pasta. Germans enjoy *spaetzle* and Poles have *pierogi;* various forms of noodles made with either rice or soy flour exist in the Orient. Pasta means "paste" in Italian. Wheat flour is combined with water or milk to make Italian pasta in a wide variety of shapes. Often an egg is added, but doughs made from flour and eggs only are generally called *noodles.* Pastas may be colored with spinach (green), beet juice or tomato paste (red) and squid ink (charcoal gray). They are available in both dried and fresh forms and are easy to make.

To cook pasta, boil salted water rapidly and add the dry or fresh pasta. Cook *al dente* which means "to the teeth" or crisp-tender. Drain and serve with sauces and cheese.

COWBOY POTATOES

8 slices bacon, diced
2 medium onions, diced
8 medium potatoes, sliced
1/2 teaspoon salt
1/4 teaspoon pepper
2 cups Cheddar cheese, shredded

Dutch Oven and At Home

Heat a 12-inch Dutch oven over 12 to 15 hot coals. Sauté the bacon; remove bacon and set aside. Pour off all but 1 tablespoon of drippings. Sauté onions until soft and add potatoes, salt and pepper. Cook, covered, 35 to 40 minutes, until potatoes are tender, stirring occasionally. Stir in bacon and sprinkle with shredded cheese. Let it rest, covered, until cheese is melted. Serves 6 to 8.

AROMATIC COUSCOUS

Your camping trip becomes an African safari, because *couscous* is a staple in North African cuisine. It is a semolina or cracked wheat that may become porridge at breakfast, a salad served with a dressing, or sweetened for a dessert. Main-dish combinations are endless.

2 1/4 cups chicken or vegetable broth
2 tablespoons butter or margarine
1 1/2 cups couscous
1/4 cup green onions, chopped
1/8 teaspoon cumin
1/4 teaspoon coriander
1 (2-inch-long rind) of 1/2 orange, cut into thin strips,
    or "zest"

Camp Stove and At Home

In a medium saucepan, heat broth to boiling. Add butter or margarine, couscous, green onions, cumin, coriander and orange zest. Cover and turn off the heat. Let it rest, covered, 10 to 20 minutes. Serves 4 to 6.

Dutch Oven

Heat a 12-inch Dutch oven over 12 to 15 hot coals. Add broth and heat until boiling. Stir in butter or margarine, couscous, green onions, cumin, coriander and orange zest. Cover and remove from coals. Let it rest, covered, 10 to 20 minutes. Serves 4 to 6.

• A more exotic version might be to add dried fruit and nuts— for example, 1/4 cup chopped dried apricots or figs and 1/4 cup sliced almonds. These additions make this wonderfully delicious!

BAKED YAMS

These taste almost like candy when prepared with melted butter or margarine, brown sugar and cinnamon.

4 medium yams, pierced
1/4 cup (1/2 stick) butter or margarine
1/2 cup brown sugar
Cinnamon

Dutch Oven

Heat a 12-inch Dutch oven over 9 hot coals. Arrange 4 jar rings evenly spaced on the bottom. Place each whole, pierced yam on top of canning jar rings. Cover with Dutch oven lid and place 15 hot coals on top. Cook, covered, 30 minutes, turning yams over once.

Cut yams in half lengthwise, fluff the center with a fork and add butter or margarine, brown sugar and cinnamon. Cook, covered, 10 to 15 minutes more, if needed. Serves 4 to 8.

At Home

On the rack in the oven, bake whole, pierced yams at 350°F. until tender, about 30 minutes. Cut in half lengthwise and add butter or margarine, brown sugar and cinnamon. Serves 4 to 8.

• Other toppings might include maple syrup, honey or apricot jam.

• Serve one half or whole to each person, depending on the yam's size and how hungry they are.

BROWN RICE PILAF

2 tablespoons butter or margarine
1 small onion, minced
1 carrot, minced
8 cloves garlic, peeled and crushed
2 cups brown rice
1 lemon
6 cups chicken or vegetable broth

Camp Stove and At Home

In a large skillet, melt butter or margarine; add onion, carrot and garlic and cook for 5 minutes. Add rice, juice of 1 lemon and broth. Cook, covered, on low heat, for 45 to 55 minutes, or until all liquid is absorbed. Serves 6 to 8.

Dutch Oven

Heat a 12-inch Dutch oven over 9 hot coals. Melt butter or margarine and add onion, carrot and garlic; cook for 5 minutes. Stir in rice and cook 5 more minutes. Add juice of 1 lemon and broth. Cover with Dutch oven lid and place 15 hot coals on top. Cook, covered, 50 to 60 minutes, or until all liquid is absorbed. Serves 6 to 8.

BAKED BUTTERNUT SQUASH

2 tablespoons butter or margarine
1 large butternut squash, cut in half and seeded (see •)
1/4 teaspoon salt
1/8 teaspoon pepper
1/4 cup pure maple syrup
Cinnamon sugar

Camp Stove and At Home

In a large skillet, melt butter or margarine; arrange squash, cut side down. Cook, covered, on low heat 35 to 45 minutes, until squash is tender. Turn over, salt and pepper and drizzle maple syrup or sprinkle cinnamon sugar into the cut side of squash. Serves 4.

Dutch Oven

Line a 12-inch Dutch oven with aluminum foil. Heat over 9

hot coals. Add butter or margarine and place squash, cut side down, on the foil. Cover with a Dutch oven lid and place 15 hot coals on top. Cook, covered, 35 to 45 minutes, or until squash is tender. Turn over, salt and pepper and drizzle maple syrup or sprinkle cinnamon sugar into the cut side of squash. Serves 4.

Foil

In a double layer of heavy-duty aluminum foil, wrap squash, cut side down. Add butter or margarine and wrap using the drugstore wrap (page 52). Place package onto a bed of hot coals and cook 30 to 40 minutes, turning over halfway. Let it rest 10 minutes before unwrapping. Turn over, salt and pepper and drizzle maple syrup or sprinkle cinnamon sugar into the cut side of squash. Serves 4.

At Home

In a baking dish, melt butter or margarine; arrange squash, cut side down. Cover with aluminum foil and bake at 350°F. for 35 to 45 minutes, until squash is tender. Turn over, salt and pepper and drizzle maple syrup or sprinkle cinnamon sugar into the cut side of squash. Serves 4.

• Any variety of winter squash (for example—acorn, blue hubbard or banana) may be substituted.

• Seeds from squash, pumpkin, sunflowers, etc., can be saved and roasted in a hot Dutch oven or in a baking pan.

To make *roasted seeds*, clean seeds and dry on a paper towel. Season with melted butter or margarine, Worcestershire sauce and salt. Bake at 325°F., stirring occasionally, for 45 minutes to 1 hour, until cooked to desired doneness.

SPANISH RICE

3 tablespoons olive oil
1 green pepper, diced
6 cloves garlic, minced
1 (15-ounce) can crushed tomatoes
2 cups rice, uncooked
1 teaspoon salt
2 1/2 cups water
1/8 teaspoon saffron powder (optional)

Camp Stove and At Home
In a large frying pan, heat oil with green pepper and garlic. Cook until soft and add tomatoes. Cook for 5 minutes, stirring occasionally. Add rice, salt, water and saffron, blending well. Cook, covered, 15 to 25 minutes, or until rice has absorbed liquid. Serves 4 to 6.

Dutch Oven
Heat a 12-inch Dutch oven over 12 to 15 hot coals. Heat oil with green pepper and garlic; cook until soft and add tomatoes. Cook, stirring occasionally, for 5 minutes. Add rice, salt, water and saffron, blending well. Cook, covered, 15 to 25 minutes, or until rice has absorbed liquid. Serves 4 to 6.

GREEN BEANS IN MARINARA SAUCE

Marinara sauce is a highly seasoned Italian tomato sauce made with onions, garlic and oregano. It can be served on pasta, meats and pizza.

3 tablespoons olive oil
1 onion, quartered and sliced
1 green pepper, cut into strips
1 (28-ounce) jar marinara sauce or tomato sauce
2 tablespoons sugar
3 (15-ounce) cans whole green beans, drained

Camp Stove and At Home
In a large skillet, heat oil and sauté onion and green pepper until soft. Add marinara sauce and sugar and bring to a boil. Add green beans and simmer 10 to 12 minutes. Serves 4 to 6.

Dutch Oven

Heat a 12-inch Dutch oven over 12 to 15 hot coals. When hot, add oil and sauté onion and green pepper until soft. Add marinara sauce and sugar and bring to a boil. Add green beans and cook for 10 to 12 minutes. Serves 4 to 6.

• Precooked, trimmed fresh green beans can be substituted for canned.

VEGETABLE STEW

Most people cut vegetables for stews the same way. If you vary slices by cutting some on the diagonal, some thick and others thin, it will make your stew more attractive and appetizing.

> **3 cups vegetable or chicken broth**
> **1 cup cauliflower, cut into florets**
> **1 cup carrots, peeled and sliced**
> **1 large onion, peeled and sliced**
> **1 (15-ounce) can whole green beans, drained**
> **2 potatoes, peeled and quartered**
> **1 (1.25-ounce) package white sauce mix**
> **1 cup Cheddar cheese, shredded**

Camp Stove and At Home

In a large saucepan, heat broth and add cauliflower, carrots, onions, green beans and potatoes. Simmer on low heat for 20 minutes, or until potatoes are tender and broth has been reduced. Remove vegetables and set aside. Whisk in white sauce mix until smooth; bring to a boil and sprinkle with cheese. Pour sauce onto vegetables to serve. Serves 6.

Dutch Oven

Heat a 12-inch Dutch oven over 12 to 15 hot coals. Heat broth and add cauliflower, carrots, onions, green beans and potatoes. Cook for 20 minutes, or until potatoes are tender and broth has been reduced. Remove vegetables and set aside. Whisk in white sauce mix until smooth; bring to a boil and sprinkle with cheese. Pour sauce onto vegetables to serve. Serves 6.

MUSHROOM STUFFING

This stuffing is delicious in Stuffed Shrimp in Garlic and Herb Butter (page 154).

1/2 pound white mushrooms, cleaned

1 green onion

2 cups fresh bread crumbs, freshly ground

2 to 3 cloves garlic, crushed

1/2 medium onion

1/4 cup fresh parsley

1/4 cup fresh thyme or oregano, or 1 tablespoon dried thyme or oregano

1 egg

1/4 teaspoon salt

1/8 teaspoon pepper

In a food processor bowl, chop mushrooms and stems, green onion, bread crumbs, garlic, onion, parsley and thyme or oregano together; pulse quickly, creating a coarse meal. Add egg, salt and pepper. Place in a small bowl or plastic self-sealing bag and refrigerate until ready to use. Do not keep for more than 2 days. Makes 2 cups.

• This may be prepared at home before taking it with you.

• A *plastic egg carton* (page 101) is available at sporting goods stores. It is a handy container for toting prepared stuffed mushrooms ready for cooking.

To Crush Garlic—

The easiest way to *crush garlic* is to first place the side of a French or chef's knife on top of a garlic clove. Using the side of your fist, hit the side of the knife. Take care not to cut your fingers. Any knife will work but the wide blade is best. The outer peel comes off in the same step and the garlic is ready to use. Once you learn to do this, you'll never do it any other way.

MEDITERRANEAN ORZO PILAF

Orzo is Italian for barley and is a popular Greek pasta. It is the only form of pasta that can be cooked in a small amount of water, which it absorbs.

3 tablespoons butter or margarine
1 cup orzo
3 cups chicken broth
1/2 cup Parmesan cheese, shredded

Camp Stove and At Home

In a large skillet on medium heat, melt butter or margarine and add orzo. Cook, stirring constantly, until orzo turns golden, about 6 to 8 minutes. Add broth and cook, covered, on low heat 35 minutes, or until all liquid is absorbed. Before serving, sprinkle with Parmesan cheese. Serves 4 to 6.

Dutch Oven

Heat a 12-inch Dutch oven over 12 to 15 hot coals. Melt butter or margarine and add orzo. Cook, stirring constantly, until orzo turns golden, about 6 to 8 minutes. Add broth and cook, covered, 35 to 40 minutes, or until all the liquid is absorbed. Before serving, sprinkle with Parmesan cheese. Serves 4 to 6.
• The real outdoor gourmet might add fresh mint, feta cheese and pine nuts in place of the Parmesan cheese.

About Pilaf—

Pilaf, a rice or bulgur dish from the Near East, usually starts by first browning the rice in butter or oil before cooking it in stock. Seasonings can be adapted using your favorite spices. Other ingredients such as chopped cooked vegetables, meat, seafood, or poultry can be added. It may be served as a side dish or a main dish. In India it is often spiced with curry.

PROVENCALE TOMATOES

When harvesting your first home-grown tomatoes, don't neglect this fabulous recipe. You will never want to use canned tomatoes again.

6 small ripe tomatoes, stemmed and cut in half
1/4 cup fresh parsley, finely chopped
1/4 cup fresh basil, finely chopped
6 to 8 cloves garlic, minced
1 teaspoon salt
1/4 teaspoon pepper
3 tablespoons olive oil
Baguette slices, grilled

Sprinkle tomato halves on the cut side with herbs, garlic, salt and pepper. Set aside.

Camp Stove and At Home

In a large skillet, heat oil until hot. Arrange tomatoes with cut side up. Cook 10 minutes; turn over and flatten with spatula. Cook 5 to 10 minutes longer, until tomatoes are soft. Serve on grilled slices of baguette. Serves 6.

Dutch Oven Lid

Place the lid of a 12-inch Dutch oven upside down on a lid holder over 12 to 15 hot coals. When lid is hot, add oil to lid. Arrange tomatoes herb side up. Cook 10 minutes; turn over and flatten with spatula. Cook 10 minutes longer, until tomatoes are soft. Serve on grilled slices of baguette. Serves 6.

• Large tomatoes may be sliced instead of halved.

• Substitute **dried herbs** if fresh are not available. Use 1 tablespoon of dried herbs for the 1/4 cup of fresh herbs.

CHAPTER 15

Butters, Rubs, Marinades, Sauces and Dressings

T he use of butters, rubs, marinades, sauces and dressings in meal preparation influences the flavor and tenderness of meats, poultry, fish and vegetables. A marinade or rub is easy to prepare and the enhanced flavor is always worth it. For convenience I use plastic self-sealing bags to mix marinades. Add meat to the bag and marinate before cooking. Most of these marinades and rubs can be prepared at home in advance of your trip outdoors. I've also included ideas for easy sauces, blended butters and tasty vinaigrettes.

Marinades and rubs add the "personality" to meats and can be created in a variety of flavors, from teriyaki to southwestern. Remember to use safe food-handling guidelines when cooking outdoors. Always marinate raw meats in your refrigerator or cooler. Never reserve marinades for serving unless you bring them to a boil first. Always wash your hands with soap and hot water when handling uncooked poultry to avoid cross-contamination.

BOUQUET GARNI

Bouquet garni is a blend of complementary herbs or vegetables tied together or placed in a cheesecloth bag and used to flavor soups, stews and broth. Remove herbs before serving.

1 (3-inch) piece of leek, bulb end slashed
1 (3-inch) piece of celery
2 bay leaves
6 cloves
1 sprig fresh thyme, or 1/2 teaspoon dried thyme

Wrap leek, celery, bay leaves, cloves and thyme in a piece of cheesecloth and tie. Refrigerate until ready to use. Drop into broth, sauce or any liquid to enhance flavor. Remove before serving.

• Cracked peppercorns can be used to add a peppery taste.

BEURRE MANIE OR KNEADED BUTTER

A basic component of French cooking, which translates as "kneaded butter or margarine," is mixed with flour to bind pan-reduced sauces. The amounts vary depending on the end use. These proportions are correct for a *medium white sauce.*

4 tablespoons (1/2 stick) butter or margarine, softened
6 tablespoons all-purpose flour

In a small bowl, blend butter or margarine and flour evenly to make a paste. To thicken a sauce, use 2 tablespoons beurre manie for every 2 to 3 cups of liquid.

In a saucepan, heat liquids on low heat until hot, whisk in the beurre manie and cook a few minutes, stirring well, until the sauce has thickened. Makes 1/2 cup.

HERBED BUTTER

A great topping for grilled meats, seafood and vegetables.

1 1/2 cups (3 sticks) butter or margarine, softened
3 tablespoons fresh thyme, minced
3 tablespoons fresh parsley, minced
3 tablespoons fresh tarragon, minced

In a small bowl, blend butter or margarine, thyme, parsley and tarragon until evenly mixed. Refrigerate, covered, until ready to use. Herbed butter or margarine keeps 5 or 6 days. Add 1 tablespoon to meats, seafood and vegetables. Makes 1 1/2 cups.

• The longer herbed butter is stored in the refrigerator, the more the flavors blend.

GARLIC AND HERB BUTTER

This is excellent on a grilled steak or sautéed shellfish.

1 1/2 cups (3 sticks) butter or margarine, softened
2 tablespoons green onions, finely minced
4 cloves garlic, crushed
3 to 4 tablespoons fresh parsley, finely chopped
Dash of lemon juice

In a small bowl, blend butter or margarine, green onions, garlic, parsley and lemon juice together to form a smooth paste. Refrigerate, covered, until ready to use. It will keep 5 to 6 days. Add 1 to 2 tablespoons, or as desired, to vegetables, meats and seafood. Makes 1 1/2 cups.

About Butters—

An easy way to store and use butters is to shape them on plastic wrap into a log about the size of a stick of butter. Wrap completely in plastic wrap and chill until firm. To use, slice off one tablespoon at a time and add to hot meat, poultry or seafood.

RED HOT BUTTER

My friend Susan can never get enough "fire" into her cooking, but this is a "hot" start.

1 1/2 cups (3 sticks) butter or margarine, softened
1 teaspoon cayenne pepper
1 teaspoon paprika
Tabasco, as desired

In a small bowl, blend butter or margarine, cayenne, paprika and tabasco, mixing until smooth. Refrigerate, covered, and use within 5 to 6 days. Makes 1 1/2 cups.

• Place a dollop of this butter or margarine on grilled fish, or use it to baste a shrimp kabob. Grilled meats and other seafood can be enhanced with this seasoned butter or margarine, especially if you like a hot southwest flavor.

CILANTRO BUTTER

1/4 cup (1/2 stick) butter or margarine, softened
3 tablespoons fresh cilantro, minced
1/2 lemon
1 teaspoon lemon zest (page 186)
1/4 teaspoon salt
Dash pepper

In a small bowl, combine butter, cilantro, juice of 1/2 lemon, zest, salt and pepper to form a smooth paste. Refrigerate, covered, until ready to use. It will keep 5 to 6 days. Add 1 tablespoon, or as desired, to vegetables, meats and seafood. Makes 1/2 cup.

About Cilantro—

Cilantro is also called Chinese parsley and coriander. It has a definite pungent fragrance and flavor and is widely used in Asian and Mexican cooking because of its distinct flavor, which lends itself to highly spiced food. It can be found fresh year-round in most produce sections of the supermarket or dried with the spices.

BARBECUE SAUCE

1/2 cup ketchup
2 tablespoons lemon juice
2 tablespoons brown sugar
2 tablespoons soy sauce
1 teaspoon garlic powder

In a l-cup covered jar, combine ketchup, lemon juice, brown sugar, soy sauce and garlic powder. Shake well, covered, to blend. Use on meats or poultry. Makes 3/4 cup.

About Rubs—

Rubs have become a "fashionable" way of seasoning meat before cooking instead of marinating. You might like to try combining all of your favorite seasonings and herbs into one mix. Don't hesitate to add a little spark such as cayenne. Added before cooking, this mixture greatly enhances the flavor of meats and poultry and is a good way to introduce your family to new flavors and tastes. Rubs are used both wet and dry. A commercial rub I am especially fond of has a high sugar and salt content, which makes it especially delicious.

DRY RUB FOR POULTRY OR DUCK

The smell of poultry rubbed with these aromats roasting in a Dutch oven is a real appetite booster.

1 tablespoon onion powder
1 tablespoon garlic powder
1 teaspoon celery salt
3 tablespoons paprika
1 teaspoon chili powder
1/2 teaspoon ground nutmeg or 2 teaspoons rosemary,
    crushed
Oil or butter or margarine, melted

In a covered jar, blend onion powder, garlic powder, celery salt, paprika, chili powder and either nutmeg or rosemary. Rinse the poultry and pat dry; rub with oil or melted butter and sprinkle dry rub all over. Roast poultry as usual. Store unused portion in a closed spice jar. This will flavor 5 pounds of poultry.

DRY RUB FOR BEEF OR PORK

3/4 tablespoon paprika
2 tablespoons onion powder
1/8 teaspoon cayenne pepper
1/2 tablespoon thyme
1/2 tablespoon oregano
2 tablespoons garlic powder
1 teaspoon crushed red pepper, optional
1/2 teaspoon white pepper
1 teaspoon salt

In a covered jar, blend together paprika, onion powder, cayenne, thyme, oregano, garlic powder, red pepper, white pepper and salt. Shake well to blend. Sprinkle on meat and rub all over it. Refrigerate meat, covered, 4 to 48 hours before cooking. Store unused portion in a closed spice jar and use as needed. This recipe makes enough to flavor 5 pounds of meat.

WET RUB FOR BEEF AND PORK

1/2 cup olive oil
1/4 cup ketchup
1/4 cup lite soy sauce
2 tablespoons lime juice
2 tablespoons paprika
2 tablespoons dried onion, minced
1 teaspoon garlic powder

In a covered glass jar, blend oil, ketchup, soy sauce, lime juice, paprika, dried onion and garlic powder; baste beef evenly with the rub. Place meat in a 1-gallon plastic self-sealing bag and refrigerate 4 to 24 hours before cooking. Baste the meat as it cooks on the grill. Store unused rub in a covered glass jar. This will flavor up to 5 pounds of meat.

WET RUB FOR POULTRY

Duck, pheasant and game hens as well as chicken and turkey
are delicious with this rub. Alter the ingredients if you want to
substitute favorites.

1/2 cup olive oil
1 teaspoon garlic powder
1 1/2 teaspoons ground cumin
1 teaspoon tarragon
1/2 teaspoon ground thyme
1 tablespoon honey
1/4 teaspoon cayenne
1/2 teaspoon white pepper

In a covered glass jar, blend olive oil, garlic powder, cumin,
tarragon, thyme, honey, cayenne, and pepper; baste poultry
evenly with the rub. Place meat in a 1-gallon plastic self-sealing bag and refrigerate 4 to 24 hours before cooking. Baste the
poultry evenly as it cooks on the grill. Store unused rub in a
covered glass jar. This will flavor up to 5 pounds of poultry.

MARINADE FOR CHEESE

Great flavor for a cheese appetizer or snack. You will want to
make this often.

3/4 cup extra virgin olive oil
1/2 tablespoon coarsely ground pepper
1/2 tablespoon garlic paste, or 1 clove garlic, crushed
1/2 tablespoon onion powder
4 to 5 sprigs fresh mint or basil (left whole)
1 (1-pound) package soft white cheese, such as
    Camembert, Gouda, Brie, Muenster or
    mozzarella, sliced in 1-by-2-inch serving pieces

In a 1-gallon plastic self-sealing bag, blend olive oil, ground
pepper, garlic paste, onion powder and fresh mint or basil; add
cheese. Refrigerate and use within 1 week. Serves 6 to 8.

About Marinades—

Marinades help to tenderize less-tender cuts of meat by marinating or soaking in an acid-based sauce containing lemon or other citrus juices, vinegar, wine or tomato juice. Before cooking, pierce the meat with a fork and add to a 1-gallon plastic self-sealing storage bag. Pour marinade over the meat and refrigerate at least 8 hours, turning meat over occasionally.

MARINADE FOR BEEF

1/2 cup ketchup
1/2 cup olive oil
1/2 lemon
1/4 cup lite soy sauce
1 tablespoon paprika
1 tablespoon fresh thyme, finely chopped
1 tablespoon fresh oregano, finely chopped
1 tablespoon onion powder
6 cloves garlic, peeled and crushed

In a covered glass jar, blend ketchup, olive oil, juice of 1/2 lemon, soy sauce, paprika, thyme, oregano, onion powder and garlic. Pour over meat in a 1-gallon plastic self-sealing bag. Refrigerate 4 to 24 hours, turning over occasionally. This is enough marinade for 5 pounds of beef.

ORIENTAL MARINADE

1/4 cup oil
1/4 cup lite soy sauce
1/4 cup sherry (optional)
4 cloves garlic, peeled and crushed, or 1 tablespoon
    garlic paste
1 tablespoon fresh ginger, finely minced
1/3 teaspoon coarsely ground pepper
2 teaspoons sugar

In a 1-gallon plastic self-sealing bag, blend oil, soy sauce, sherry, garlic, ginger, ground pepper and sugar. Add meat and refrigerate 2 to 3 hours, turning over occasionally. This recipe makes enough marinade for 2 pounds of meat.

MARINADE FOR PORK AND POULTRY

1/2 lemon
1/2 cup olive oil
1 teaspoon onion powder
6 cloves garlic, peeled and crushed
1/4 cup fresh thyme, finely chopped
1/4 cup fresh oregano, finely chopped
4 bay leaves
6 cloves
1/2 teaspoon salt
1 teaspoon freshly ground pepper

In a covered glass jar, blend juice of 1/2 lemon, olive oil, onion powder, garlic, thyme, oregano, bay leaves, cloves, salt and pepper. Pour over pork or poultry in a 1-gallon plastic self-sealing bag. Refrigerate 4 to 24 hours, turning over occasionally. This is enough marinade for 5 pounds of pork or poultry.
• Substitute 1 tablespoon dried herbs for 1/4 cup fresh herbs.

TERIYAKI MARINADE

An excellent marinade for meat sticks, spare ribs, chicken and steak. The sesame-seed oil really makes it.

1 cup lite soy sauce
1/2 cup sugar
1/2 cup water
1/2 tablespoon fresh ginger, shredded
1 clove garlic, peeled and crushed
2 green onions, chopped
1 tablespoon sesame-seed oil

In a medium saucepan, heat soy sauce, sugar and water, and boil until sugar dissolves, about 5 minutes. Add ginger, garlic, green onions and sesame-seed oil. Refrigerate, covered, in a 1-pint glass jar. This recipe makes enough marinade for 3 pounds of meat.

BALSAMIC VINAIGRETTE DRESSING

Use as a mild salad dressing or an excellent dip for focaccia or Italian bread.

1/3 cup balsamic vinegar
2/3 cup extra virgin olive oil
1/3 cup Parmesan cheese, freshly shredded
1 teaspoon coarsely ground black pepper

In a 2-cup measure, blend vinegar, olive oil, cheese and pepper. Refrigerate, covered, in a glass jar up to 10 days. Makes 1 1/3 cups.

BASIC VINAIGRETTE DRESSING

2 teaspoons Dijon mustard
1/4 cup red wine vinegar
3/4 cup extra virgin olive oil
1 teaspoon salt
1/2 teaspoon pepper

In a 2-cup measure, blend mustard and vinegar; whisk in olive oil, salt and pepper. Refrigerate, covered, in a glass jar up to 10 days. Makes 1 cup.

GARLIC AND HERB VINAIGRETTE DRESSING

2 teaspoons Dijon mustard
1/4 cup red wine vinegar
1/4 cup extra virgin olive oil
2 to 3 cloves garlic, peeled and crushed
2 tablespoons fresh herbs, such as rosemary, thyme, basil or oregano, finely minced
1/2 teaspoon salt
1/8 teaspoon pepper

In a 1-cup measure, dissolve mustard in vinegar and whisk in olive oil. Add garlic, herbs, salt and pepper, mixing well. Pour over your salad immediately or set aside to serve later. Makes 3/4 cup.

About Vinaigrette—

A basic oil and vinegar, lemon juice or wine salad dressing brings out the flavors of salad greens and other cold vegetables, meat or fish dishes. Vinaigrette is usually three parts oil to one part vinegar, lemon juice or wine and salt and pepper. Other ingredients often added are herbs, mustard, onions, shallots, spices, etc.

LEMON VINAIGRETTE DRESSING

1/3 cup lemon juice
2/3 cup extra virgin olive oil
1 teaspoon cumin
1 teaspoon coriander
1/2 teaspoon salt
1/8 teaspoon pepper

In a 2-cup measure, combine lemon juice, olive oil, cumin, coriander, salt and pepper. Whisk well and pour over your salad immediately. Makes 1 cup.

AVOCADO DRESSING

A wonderful dressing with seafood salad or as a dip for chips.

2 very ripe avocados, peeled and mashed
1/4 cup lemon juice
3/4 cup extra virgin olive oil
1 clove garlic, crushed, or 1 teaspoon garlic paste
1 teaspoon onion paste
1/2 teaspoon salt
Pinch of cayenne pepper
2 tablespoons honey

In a 2-cup measure, combine avocados, lemon juice, olive oil, garlic paste, onion paste, salt, pepper and honey. If dressing is too thick, thin with a little more lemon juice and olive oil. Makes 2 cups.

CHAMPAGNE VINAIGRETTE DRESSING

2 teaspoons Dijon mustard
1/4 cup champagne vinegar
1 cup extra virgin olive oil
1 green onion, minced

In a 2-cup measure, blend mustard, vinegar, olive oil and green onion. Pour over your salad immediately or set aside to serve later. Whisk briefly before serving. Makes 1 1/4 cups.

LEMON DILL DRESSING FOR FISH

2 tablespoons dill weed
1/4 cup fresh chives, finely chopped
2 tablespoons lemon juice
1/4 cup sour cream
1/2 cup mayonnaise
1 teaspoon honey
Salt
Pepper

In a 2-cup measure, blend dill, chopped chives, lemon juice, sour cream, mayonnaise, honey, salt and pepper. Chill before serving with poached fish or poultry. Makes 1 1/4 cups.

CREAM SAUCE FOR FRUIT

Zest is the colored outer layer only of oranges, lemons and limes. A knife called a "zester" makes this job easier.

1 (8-ounce) package cream cheese or mascarpone
   cheese, softened
1/3 cup heavy cream
1/2 cup powdered sugar
Zest of 1 lemon or 1 orange
1/4 cup fresh lemon juice or orange juice

In a small deep glass bowl, whip cream cheese and heavy cream until soft and fluffy. Add sugar, zest and juice, and cream well. Refrigerate until needed. Makes approximately 1 2/3 cups.

CHAPTER 16

Breads and Doughs

As mentioned in the introduction, the earliest impact outdoor cooking had on me was when my father baked biscuits in a Dutch oven. Since then, all my favorite bread, muffin and other dough recipes have been adapted for multiple methods of outdoor cooking. It's a lot easier to be creative outdoors with dough than you might imagine. One of the simplest, most satisfying and fun recipes is **Bread on a Stick** (page 44).

More elaborate breads, muffins and rolls can be easily prepared while cooking other courses of your meal. I've included recipes for **Herb and Cheese Focaccia, Quick Scones** and **Sourdough** (pages 192, 194 and 196), just to show you how easy it is to create these taste sensations outdoors. Don't forget to bring plenty of butter or margarine and jam.

Ready-to-Eat and Prepared Foods

When you're outside or camping, almost nothing beats the aroma of hot bread baking over the hot coals. With a Dutch oven, you can bake bread and several other exciting items that require no preparation at all. Many are found in the freezer case at your supermarket.

Frozen Dough:

- Orange rolls
- Cinnamon rolls
- Texas rolls
- Whole wheat rolls

The newest items are "no-thaw," freezer-to-table doughs that are ready in 30 minutes. Called "anytime rolls," they include:

- Buttermilk rolls
- Caramel rolls
- Parker House rolls
- Chocolate cinnamon rolls
- Cinnamon rolls
- Orange rolls

Baked in their own pan, they can be popped into the Dutch oven, baked and iced with the included frosting. Enjoy!

Brown-and-serve rolls, found in the baked bread section of your supermarket, can be baked on your **camp stove** or **grill.** Because they may stick to your stove or grill, either brush the rolls before baking with butter or oil or oil the grill.

ALL-PURPOSE BAKING MIX

This mix makes muffins, quick breads or pancakes by adding egg, milk or buttermilk and some fruit, nuts and spices.

4 cups all-purpose flour
1/3 cup sugar
1/4 cup baking powder
1 1/2 teaspoons salt
1 cup (2 sticks) butter or margarine or shortening

In a large mixing bowl, blend flour, sugar, baking powder and salt; cut butter or margarine or shortening into the dry mix using either 2 knives, a pastry blender or your fingers. Store in a 1-gallon plastic self-sealing bag up to 2 to 3 months in a cool, dry place.

LARGE CAKE MUFFINS

2 1/2 cups baking mix (page 188) or Bisquick

1 egg, beaten

1 cup milk or buttermilk (see •)

1 cup of fruit such as blueberries, cranberries, raspberries, fresh shredded apple, chopped dried apricots, etc.

1 teaspoon spice such as cinnamon, nutmeg, cardamom or ginger

1/2 cup walnuts, chopped (optional)

• Adding dry milk or buttermilk when preparing the baking mix allows you to add water (not fresh milk) when using.

In a medium mixing bowl, combine baking mix, egg, milk or buttermilk, fruit, spices and walnuts; stir just until moistened. Pour into muffin cups lined with baking papers.

Dutch Oven

Heat a 12-inch Dutch oven over 9 hot coals. Arrange 3 canning jar rings or a Dutch oven rack in the bottom. Pour one-half of the batter into a buttered, floured 9-inch cake pan and set on the rack. Cover with Dutch oven lid and place 15 hot coals on the top. Bake, covered, 15 to 20 minutes, or until a toothpick inserted in the center comes out clean. Repeat with remaining batter (see •). Serves 10 to 12.

• A 6-cup muffin pan will fit nicely into a 12-inch Dutch oven. Foil muffin cups are also available. Add baking papers to each muffin cup and fill two-thirds with batter. Place on canning jar rings or a Dutch oven rack and follow the above directions for baking in a Dutch oven.

At Home

Preheat oven to 350°F. Line muffin cups with baking papers and fill two-thirds with batter. Bake 15 to 20 minutes, or until evenly browned and top springs back when touched in the center. Serves 10 to 12.

• Do not overmix or your muffins will have "tunnels."

• For a more *savory muffin*, add shredded cheese, cooked bacon bits, chili peppers and/or herbs instead of fruit.

SPOON BREAD

3 strips bacon, diced
2 (8-ounce) packages corn muffin mix, unprepared
2 teaspoons baking powder
1 (4-ounce) package bleu cheese, crumbled (optional)
4 eggs, beaten
1 1/2 cups milk
2 tablespoons butter or margarine, melted

Dutch Oven

Heat a 12-inch Dutch oven over 9 hot coals and sauté bacon until well cooked. Pour off all but 1 tablespoon of drippings. In a mixing bowl, add corn muffin mix, baking powder and cheese. In a small bowl, blend eggs, milk and butter or margarine and add to dry ingredients. Pour batter into hot drippings. Cover with Dutch oven lid with 15 hot coals on top. Bake, covered, 20 to 30 minutes, or until evenly browned and top springs back in the center. Serves 8 to 12.

At Home

Preheat oven to 350°F. In a large skillet, sauté bacon until well cooked. Pour off all but 1 tablespoon of drippings. In a mixing bowl, combine corn muffin mix, baking powder and cheese. In a small bowl, blend eggs, cream, milk and butter or margarine and add to dry ingredients. Pour batter into hot drippings or a buttered 9 x 13-inch baking dish. Bake for 20 to 30 minutes, or until evenly browned and top springs back in the center. Serves 8 to 12.

• If your skillet handle is oven-safe, bake bread in the skillet. Otherwise, use a 9 x 13-inch baking dish.

About Quick Breads—

Quick-to-make breads such as spoon bread, biscuits, coffee cake and muffins do not require kneading or rising because the leavening called for in the recipe is usually baking powder or baking soda instead of yeast or sourdough. When liquid is added to the leavening, the batter immediately rises. Double-acting baking powder has a second rising in the oven when exposed to heat. Eggs help to leaven quick breads.

COFFEE CAKE

A group activity that can involve everyone in the mixing.

1/2 cup (1 stick) butter or margarine, lightly melted
1 cup (8 ounces) sour cream
1/2 cup sugar
4 eggs, beaten
1 (18.25-ounce) box yellow cake mix
1/2 cup brown sugar
2 tablespoons cinnamon
1 cup walnuts, finely chopped
1/2 cup dried apricots, finely chopped
Vegetable oil, as needed

In a 1-gallon plastic self-sealing bag, add butter or margarine, sour cream and sugar; push out air and seal. Squeeze to mix; add eggs and squeeze well. Add dry cake mix and squeeze batter 2 to 3 minutes.

In a 1-quart plastic self-sealing bag, mix together brown sugar, cinnamon, walnuts and apricots.

Dutch Oven

Line a 12-inch Dutch oven with heavy-duty aluminum foil and heat over 9 hot coals. Cover with Dutch oven lid and place 15 hot coals on the top. Preheat for 10 minutes.

Lightly oil foil and pour half of the batter into the Dutch oven. Sprinkle with half of the topping; add remaining batter and sprinkle with the remaining topping. Cook, covered, for 40 to 50 minutes, or until a toothpick inserted into the center comes out clean. Cool 10 to 15 minutes. Lift out foil to serve. Serves 8 to 10.

At Home

Preheat oven to 350°F. Prepare batter and pour into a buttered, floured bundt pan following **Dutch oven** method. Bake 40 to 50 minutes, or until a toothpick inserted into the center comes out clean. Cool 10 to 15 minutes. To unmold, loosen sides and center with a table knife and invert onto a large cake plate. Serves 8 to 10.

PITA POCKETS

1/4 cup flour
6 large frozen rolls, thawed and doubled in volume
3 tablespoons olive oil

Grill and At Home

Lightly flour the counter. With a rolling pin, roll defrosted dough into a round, flat shape about 10 inches in diameter. Brush the dough with olive oil on both sides and place on a hot grill. Cook 45 to 60 seconds on each side until evenly browned. Remove from heat, slice in wedges to open and add filling, as desired. Serve warm or cold. Serves 8 to 12.

• Season with salt and pepper or add herbs before cooking if desired.

Pita pockets are easy and fun to fill for a quick lunch

HERB AND CHEESE FOCACCIA

You'll make this dough often to serve as an herbed bread or as the crust for pizza.

1 1/2 tablespoons dry yeast
2 tablespoons sugar
1 1/2 cups very warm water
4 tablespoons olive oil
1 teaspoon salt
1 teaspoon garlic powder
1 tablespoon Italian herbs
2 1/2 cups all-purpose flour
Vegetable or olive oil, for greasing hands
2 tablespoons olive oil
1/2 cup shredded Parmesan cheese

In a mixing bowl, combine yeast, sugar and water, and let mixture rest for 10 minutes, until yeast begins to bubble. Stir in olive oil, salt, garlic powder and herbs and 1 1/4 cups flour, mixing well. Let dough rest for 20 minutes; add remaining 1 1/4 cups flour. Oil your hands and knead the wet dough until light and elastic. Let it rise, covered with plastic wrap, until double in size (approximately 1 hour). Oil your hands again and knead the dough inside the bowl for 1 to 2 minutes.

• This dough is soft and cannot be kneaded on a counter.

Dutch Oven

Line a 12-inch Dutch oven with buttered heavy-duty aluminum foil. Lift out molded foil pan and stretch and ease the dough to fit the foil. Punch dimples into the dough with your fingers and sprinkle with 2 tablespoons of olive oil and cheese. Let it rise, covered with plastic wrap, until double in size.

Heat a 12-inch Dutch oven over 9 hot coals. Cover with Dutch oven lid and place 15 hot coals on top. Preheat for 10 to 15 minutes. Place dough on the foil inside the Dutch oven and bake, covered, for 30 to 35 minutes, or until golden brown. Cut into wedges to serve. Serves 8 to 10.

At Home

Oil a 10- to 12-inch round pizza or cake pan. Stretch and ease the dough to fit the pan. Punch dimples into the dough with your fingers and sprinkle with 2 tablespoons of olive oil and cheese. Let it rise, covered with plastic wrap, until double in size. Bake at 375°F. for 25 to 30 minutes, until golden brown. Cut into wedges to serve. Serves 8 to 10.

About Focaccia—

This is an Italian bread that is usually round and flat, liberally brushed or drizzled with olive oil and sprinkled with salt. Slits are cut into the dough surface to stuff with fresh rosemary stems or other fresh herbs before baking. It is usually eaten as a snack, appetizer or accompaniment to soups, salads or main dishes. The dough can be used as the bottom crust for pizza with your favorite toppings.

PIZZELLE CRUST

You'll treasure this special dough, which can be used anytime you want a quick, homemade bread or pizza dough.

1 tablespoon active dry yeast
1 1/2 teaspoons sugar
1 1/2 cups warm water
3 1/4 cups all-purpose flour, divided
1 1/2 teaspoons olive oil
1 teaspoon salt

In a mixing bowl, blend yeast and sugar in water and set aside for 10 minutes, until yeast begins to bubble. Add 2 cups of flour, oil and salt; stir well and set aside for 20 minutes. Add remaining 1 1/4 cups of flour to form a soft dough. Oil your hands and knead dough in the bowl for 2 minutes. Oil the bowl and turn dough over to coat it on all sides. Let it rise, covered with plastic wrap, until double in size. Cut dough into 4 equal portions. Use each portion for pizza or for the **Goat Cheese and Caramelized Onion Pizzelle** (page 158).

• Prepare ahead and freeze in four separate portions. Use on a moment's notice for appetizers or take frozen, wrapped in newspapers, with you camping. Dough will begin to rise at room temperature. It can be punched down 2 or 3 times before cooking.

• Use your favorite pizza toppings.

QUICK SCONES

A convenient way to use leftover pancake batter. Occasionally I make extra batter for these. This is one of the best scones you will ever eat—the center is never doughy.

1 cup vegetable oil for frying
4 to 6 English muffins, cut in half
2 to 3 cups prepared pancake batter
Toppings of your choice (see • next page)

Camp Stove and At Home

In a large, deep skillet, heat oil until a drop of pancake batter dropped into the skillet sizzles. With a fork, dip muffins into the pancake batter and carefully add to the hot oil. Cook on both sides until golden brown. Remove and drain on paper towels. Serve hot with toppings, as desired. Serves 4.

Dutch Oven

Heat a 12-inch Dutch oven over 12 to 15 hot coals. Heat oil until a drop of pancake batter dropped into the skillet sizzles. With a fork, dip muffins into the pancake batter and carefully add to the hot oil. Cook on both sides until golden brown. Remove and drain on paper towels. Serve hot with toppings, as desired. Serves 4.

• Serve plain or topped with sugar, powdered sugar, brown sugar, cinnamon sugar, honey, jam, jelly or syrup varieties such as strawberry, maple, caramel, etc. Another topping I enjoy is powdered sugar and fresh lemon juice.

Scones eaten while camping taste even better!

SESAME BREADSTICKS
1 (15-ounce) bag brown-and-serve breadsticks
1/2 cup (1 stick) butter or margarine, melted
1/2 cup sesame seeds

Camp Stove

Brush breadsticks with butter or margarine and roll in the sesame seeds. Preheat a cast-iron skillet, covered, on the lowest setting. Wait a few minutes; arrange breadsticks in the pan. Brown on both sides, 8 to 10 minutes, and serve immediately. Serves 8 to 12.

Dutch Oven

Heat a 12-inch Dutch oven over 9 hot coals. Brush breadsticks with butter or margarine and roll in the sesame seeds. Place in the Dutch oven and cover with Dutch oven lid. Place 15 hot coals on top and cook, covered, until evenly browned, 10 to 15 minutes. Serve immediately. Serves 8 to 12.

At Home

Preheat oven to 350°F. Brush breadsticks with butter or margarine and roll in the sesame seeds. Arrange breadsticks on a cookie sheet. Bake 6 to 8 minutes, or until golden brown, and serve immediately. Serves 8 to 12.

• Shredded cheese may be added halfway through the cooking time, if desired.

Sourdough Bread

Delicious sourdough bread—always a favorite and a winner out-of-doors—was the principal bread of the hardworking men and women who built the West. You, too, can enjoy its heartiness and flavor. Once you begin, you'll likely always want to use sourdough for baking.

In pioneer days, sourdough was developed from a culture of flour, water and wild yeast. Wild yeast is atmospheric bacteria, similar to that used for souring milk or making cottage cheese. The "starter" plus dough emerged with ingredients to create unlimited breads and biscuits. About one or two cups of starter always remains to activate new dough; that's why it is called the "starter." Today, it's easy to make a starter with flour, sugar, yeast and water.

About Containers—

The most common sourdough container for camp or home use is a 1- to 2-gallon earthenware crock with a loose-fitting lid. Plastic or glass containers with loose-fitting lids or plastic wrap work equally well. Acids from the bacterial action of the dough react on metal; thus metal containers are not recommended. It is essential that the lid or cover be loose or unsealed because the contents might explode if gas cannot expand and escape.

MAKING SOURDOUGH STARTER

Your homemade starter will work just as well as one that has been passed down through generations. Some families pride themselves on its length of time in use, and many even give their starter a name.

1 cup all-purpose flour
1/2 tablespoon dry yeast
1 teaspoon sugar
1 1/2 cups warm water

In a crock or plastic container, combine flour, yeast, sugar and warm water. Leave at room temperature for 3 days, adding 1 cup of new flour and 1/2 cup warm water each day until batter is active—odor is pungent and the surface is bubbly. This occurs from the gas released by the action of the yeast.

At this point your starter is ready to form the basis of sourdough recipes. Remember to set aside 1 to 2 cups of starter for the next batch. The amount of dough you mix will depend on the number of bread loaves or biscuits desired.

MAINTAINING SOURDOUGH STARTER

To maintain the starter, use the dough frequently. The starter will keep for several days and even weeks—by refrigerating or freezing between uses. When making a new batch of bread or pancakes, bring the starter to room temperature a day or so

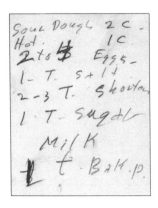

*Dad's original handwrit-
ten sourdough recipe card*

before using and let it reactivate in a warm (not hot) temperature.

To shorten rising time, mix the dough with warm water and keep it in a warm place. To **lengthen rising time**, mix the dough with cold water and keep it in a cool place until you plan to use it.

In outdoor camping areas during cold periods, the dough can be mixed with warm water and covered with insulation such as coats or bedding to "wake it up." During warm weather, mix it with cold water and store in a cool place so it will not become too active.

When the dough becomes more sour, it will not make a good finished product and should be discarded, except for a small amount to activate a new starter. Adding cultured yeast helps to renew the starter. When you begin to mix the dough, the bowl should be less than half full because it will more than double in size and may overflow the container.

Dad and his favorite Dutch ovens

MIXING BREAD AND BISCUITS

The night before or several hours prior to making bread or biscuits, add 1 cup of flour and 1/2 cup of warm water to the starter. Sourdough bread dough should be stiffer, left to rise longer, and baked longer than dough for biscuits.

The old-timers who were "packing" carried flour in a seamless or heavy flour sack and rolled the top down to the level of the flour, shaped the flour with their fingers into a bowl, poured starter into the bowl and mixed it. Today, the traditional method for making sourdough is to place flour in a deep kettle or mixing bowl and with the backs of the fingers, mold it into a bowl shape. Into this "well" pour the desired amount of activated sourdough "starter."

SOURDOUGH BREADS AND BISCUITS

Sourdough biscuits were a mainstay for many sheepherders. They may well become a mainstay for you too. The smell and the taste are incredible.

All-purpose flour to cover the bottom of a kettle or bowl

2 cups sourdough starter

1 teaspoon salt

1 teaspoon baking powder

1/4 teaspoon baking soda

1/4 cup shortening or bacon drippings, melted

2 tablespoons sugar

Combine flour, sourdough starter, salt, baking powder, baking soda, shortening or drippings and sugar, using the "well" method described above.

Knead thoroughly by folding from the outside to the center using your hands or a spoon. Make bread dough stiffer than biscuit dough. Shape into loaves, oblong or round, or biscuits. Ease dough for **bread** into a buttered loaf or round heat-proof bowl or an oiled 12-inch Dutch oven, or for **biscuits**, shape into small balls in your hand and place them side by side into a buttered or oiled 12-inch Dutch oven or cake pan. Brush the top with oil. Let them rise, covered with plastic wrap, until double in size.

Dutch Oven and At Home

Heat Dutch oven using 10 hot coals on the bottom. Cover with a Dutch oven lid and place 14 hot coals on top. Bake:

Bread loaf about 1 hour (350°F.)

Biscuits 20 to 30 minutes (350°F.)

• Bread internal temperature tested with a thermometer in the center is 200°F. when completely cooked, says Julia Child.

SOURDOUGH PANCAKES

An essential to making good pancakes is cooking them on a hot griddle. The griddle should smoke when greased or oiled, and it should sizzle if water is dropped onto it. Make a small sample cake to see if it turns golden brown instead of light brown or "whitish." A griddle which is not hot enough will not make good cakes; if it is too hot, cakes will burn. A heavy aluminum or iron griddle, a Dutch oven, or a Dutch oven lid will give pleasing results.

1 cup sourdough starter
1 cup prepared dry pancake mix or all-purpose baking mix (page 188)
2 eggs
3 tablespoons oil
1 tablespoon sugar

In a medium mixing bowl, blend sourdough starter, dry pancake mix, eggs, oil and sugar. Do not over-stir. If batter is too thick, thin with milk. Add 1/4 teaspoon baking soda if the dough is too sour. Ladle onto a hot griddle. Turn over when light brown.

Serve pancakes warm from the griddle. The quality diminishes if they are stacked or allowed to rest and cool. Makes 10 to 12.

Pancakes plus—add berries, sliced peaches, pineapple, chopped apples, nuts, raisins and bits of ham to batter for extra nutritious pancakes

CHAPTER 17

Desserts

I've saved the best for last—my award-winning desserts. This is where I have converted those nonbelievers who thought cakes, pies and ice cream were impossible to make outdoors. Some of the best cobblers and pies can be baked inside a Dutch oven—this is an easy and delicious way to use fresh fruits. Other desserts not commonly associated with grilling, such as **Shaggy Dogs** (page 50) are delicious when prepared outdoors.

One of my signature recipes is **Kick-the-Can Ice Cream** (page 92). Kids find it as much fun to make as to eat. I've included ideas for other nontraditional desserts and methods for adapting your own favorites to easy outdoor baking. Dessert recipes are also found in other chapters of the book.

BAKED APPLES

1/2 cup brown sugar
1/4 teaspoon cinnamon
1/4 teaspoon nutmeg
1/4 cup (1/2 stick) butter or margarine, melted
1/2 cup walnuts, finely chopped
1/2 cup raisins
6 cooking apples, cored

Dutch Oven

Line the bottom of a 12-inch Dutch oven with heavy-duty aluminum foil. In a small bowl, mix together sugar, cinnamon, nutmeg, butter or margarine, walnuts and raisins. Fill the cavity of each apple with 1/6 of the mixture. Arrange apples in the Dutch oven and place over 9 hot coals. Cover with Dutch oven lid and place 15 hot coals on the top. Bake, covered, for 40 to 50 minutes, or until apples are soft. Serves 6.

At Home

Follow the above **Dutch oven** directions using an oven pan or dish. Bake, covered with aluminum foil, at 350°F. for 40 to 50 minutes. Serves 6.

• For a sugar-free version, replace the sugar with a sweetener.
• Spoon some **Kick-the-Can Ice Cream** (page 92) and pan drippings on top before serving.
• Score though peel around the center of the apple before filling to prevent shriveling during cooking.
• My friend Barbara likes to fill the core with red hots and sugar cubes. The red hots melt during cooking—yum!

DUMP CAKE

1 (29-ounce) can sliced peaches with juice
1 (18.25-ounce) white or yellow cake mix
1/4 cup (1/2 stick) butter or margarine, cold

Dutch Oven

Into a 12-inch Dutch oven, pour peaches and juice. On the top of the peaches, evenly spread the dry cake mix; stir slightly to moisten. Dot the top with butter or margarine.

Heat the Dutch oven over 9 hot coals. Cover with Dutch

oven lid and place 15 hot coals on the top to create a 325°F. oven. Bake, covered, 30 to 40 minutes, or until top is golden brown and a toothpick inserted in the center comes out clean. Serves 8 to 10.

• Canned pineapple, cherries, apples and other fruits or unthickened pie filling may be substituted for peaches. If you use thickened pie filling, add 1 can of lemon-lime soda pop.

• Chopped nuts can also be sprinkled over the top.

• The flavor of the cake may also be varied by selecting a different mix and fruit. Cherry pie filling is delicious with chocolate cake.

• The Dutch oven can be lined with heavy-duty aluminum foil for easy cleaning.

PINEAPPLE CARAMEL CANDY

A dream of a combination and the easiest recipe for candy you'll ever make.

1 (15-ounce) can pineapple tidbits, well drained
1 (7.25-ounce) jar caramel topping for ice cream
1 cup angel flake coconut
8 squares graham crackers, crumbled in a plastic self-
sealing bag

Camp Stove and At Home

In a large frying pan on low heat, warm caramel; add pineapple, coconut and crumbs. Cook 2 to 3 minutes, stirring to blend, until hot. Serves 3 to 4.

Dutch Oven

Line a 12-inch Dutch oven with heavy-duty aluminum foil and place over 12 hot coals. Pour caramel into the foil and heat until warm. Add pineapple, coconut and crumbs. Cook 2 to 3 minutes, stirring to blend, until hot. Serve over ice cream. Serves 3 to 4.

• Substitute fudge sauce if you're a chocolate lover.

CRAISIN BREAD PUDDING

A "farewell" recipe for the end of your camping trip to utilize leftover bread.

6 eggs
1/2 cup sugar
1/2 cup sour cream
1 cup half and half or milk
1/2 loaf bread
1/2 cup craisins or raisins
1/2 cup walnuts, chopped
3/4 cup brown sugar
1/2 cup (1 stick) butter or margarine, melted

Dutch Oven

In a small mixing bowl, mix together eggs, sugar, sour cream and half and half. Line a 12-inch Dutch oven with heavy-duty aluminum foil. Layer ingredients in this order: 1/2 of the bread, craisins or raisins, walnuts, premixed liquids, sugar and butter or margarine. Repeat in the same order using remaining ingredients.

Heat Dutch oven over 9 hot coals. Cover with Dutch oven lid and place 15 hot coals on the top, creating a 325°F. oven. Bake, covered, 30 to 40 minutes, or until a toothpick inserted in the center comes out clean. Serve warm. Serves 6 to 8.

At Home

Follow the above **Dutch oven** directions using a bread pan or rectangular oven dish. Bake at 325°F. for 30 to 40 minutes, or until a toothpick inserted in the center comes out clean. Serve warm. Serves 6 to 8.

• French baguette, Italian bread or any day-old bread may be used.

• Dried cherries can be substituted for the craisins or raisins.

• One-half cup white chocolate chips may be added with the craisins, if desired.

EASY BROWNIES

1 1/2 cups all-purpose flour
2 cups sugar
2/3 cup cocoa
1/2 teaspoon salt
3/4 cup vegetable oil
4 eggs
1 teaspoon vanilla
1/2 cup nuts, finely chopped

Dutch Oven

Line a 12-inch Dutch oven with heavy-duty aluminum foil and place Dutch oven over 9 hot coals. Cover with Dutch oven lid and place 15 hot coals on the top. Preheat 10 minutes.

In a medium mixing bowl, mix flour, sugar, cocoa, salt, oil, eggs, vanilla and nuts, and pour into the foil. Bake, covered, 40 to 50 minutes, or until a toothpick inserted in the center comes out clean. Cool before cutting. Serves 8 to 12.

At Home

Oil and flour a 9 x 13-inch rectangular cake pan. Preheat oven to 325°F. In a medium mixing bowl, blend flour, sugar, cocoa, salt, oil, eggs, vanilla and nuts, and pour batter into a buttered and floured pan. Bake for 30 minutes, or until a toothpick inserted in the center comes out clean. Cool before cutting. Serves 8 to 10.

PEACH MELBA

Grilled peaches, at room temperature (page 206)
1 1/2 cups raspberry or red currant syrup
1 cup heavy cream, whipped
1/2 cup toasted almond slices

Place grilled peaches in 6 bowls. Pour 1/4 cup syrup on each peach. Top with whipped cream and sprinkle with almonds to serve. Serves 4 to 6.

• Peaches can be prepared ahead of time and refrigerated.

GRILLED PEACHES

2 tablespoons butter or margarine
4 to 6 fresh peaches, peeled and halved
1/4 cup brown sugar

Camp Stove and At Home

In a large skillet, melt butter or margarine; place peach halves, cut side down, into the butter or margarine. Do not touch peaches until they are browned. Turn peaches over and brown well. Crumble brown sugar on top. When liquid and sugar form a syrup, about 10 minutes, serve warm or cold or use for **Peach Melba** (page 205). Serves 4 to 6.

Dutch Oven Lid

Place the lid of a 12-inch Dutch oven upside down on a lid holder over 12 hot coals and heat until hot.

Melt butter or margarine and place peach halves, cut side down, in butter or margarine. Do not touch peaches until they are browned. Turn peaches over and brown well. Crumble brown sugar on top. When liquid and sugar form a syrup, about 10 minutes, serve warm or cold or use for **Peach Melba** (page 205). Serves 4 to 6.

• Delicious with **Kick-the-Can Ice Cream** (page 92).

GRILLED POUND CAKE
AND BERRY COUPE

Coupe is a French description for ice cream or sherbet with a topping of fruit or whipped cream. This is scrumptious served with **Kick-the-Can Ice Cream** (page 92).

   1 (10.75-ounce) pound cake
   2 tablespoons butter or margarine, melted
   24 ounces frozen berries, as desired
   1/2 cup sugar
   2 cups whipped cream, optional

Camp Stove

Cut pound cake into 8 even slices. Brush with butter or margarine on both sides. Heat the grill section of your camp stove until very hot. Arrange slices of pound cake on the grill diagonally to make grill marks on the cake slices. Cook 1 minute on each side. Set aside.

In a large skillet, blend frozen berries and sugar over medium heat for 10 minutes, stirring occasionally, until berries are thawed and sugar is dissolved. Serve hot or cold with berry sauce spooned onto pound cake and topped with whipped cream. Serves 8.

At Home

Follow the above **camp stove** directions using a "marking" skillet (see •) to grill cake and a regular skillet to cook berries. Serves 8.

• A *"marking"* skillet has raised ribs built into the bottom of the pan so that grill marks are made on cooked foods. When grilling meats, the ribs allow drippings to drain.

S'MORES

A new variation of an old favorite that will bring a lifetime of memories.

Marshmallows
Milk **chocolate chips**
Graham crackers
Roasting sticks or skewers

With a sharp knife point, punch three slits on the outside of one end of each marshmallow and place *milk* chocolate chips, sharp end first, into the slits. Thread 2 marshmallows with chocolate chip ends together onto a stick or skewer. Roast, turning slowly, over hot coals until golden brown. Be careful not to get too close to the coals or the marshmallows will burn. Carefully slide off the skewer between two graham crackers and serve.

Make three cuts for your chocolate chips

Place two marshmallows with chips together for toasting

MIXED BERRY CRISP

Berries in season are always best. When not in season, use frozen.

1 (10-ounce) bag frozen raspberries, thawed
1 (10-ounce) bag frozen blueberries, thawed
1 (10-ounce) bag frozen boysenberries or blackberries, thawed
3/4 cup sugar

In a bowl combine berries and sugar; set aside. Prepare **Crisp Topping** (below).

Dutch Oven

Heat a 12-inch Dutch oven over 9 hot coals. Cover with Dutch oven lid and place 15 hot coals on the top. Preheat 10 minutes. Pour the berry mixture into the Dutch oven. Sprinkle **Crisp Topping** (below) evenly onto berries. Bake, covered, for 30 to 35 minutes. Serve warm or cold. Serves 6 to 8.

At Home

Follow the above **Dutch oven** directions. Cook in a baking dish at 350°F. for 30 to 35 minutes, or until golden brown. Serve warm or cold. Serves 6 to 8.

• A scoop of **Kick-the-Can Ice Cream** (page 92) makes a great complement.

CRISP TOPPING

1 cup all-purpose flour
1 cup walnuts, finely chopped
1 cup brown sugar
1 cup oatmeal
1/2 cup (1 stick) butter or margarine, melted

In a medium bowl or in a 1-quart plastic self-sealing bag, add flour, walnuts, brown sugar, oatmeal and butter or margarine, and mix. This can be prepared at home and added to the Berry Crisp (above) outdoors. Excellent on cooked fruit or added to coffee cake before baking.

MACAROON SHORTCAKE

1 1/3 cups powdered sugar
1/2 cup almonds, ground
1 cup angel flake coconut
1/2 cup all-purpose flour
1/2 teaspoon baking powder
1/4 cup (1/2 stick) butter or margarine, melted
6 egg whites, whipped into stiff peaks
1/4 cup sugar

Dutch Oven

In a large bowl, combine powdered sugar, almonds, coconut, flour and baking powder, and mix well. Add butter or margarine, stirring well, and fold in whipped egg whites.

Line a 12-inch Dutch oven with heavy-duty aluminum foil. Heat Dutch oven over 9 hot coals. Cover with Dutch oven lid and place 15 hot coals on the top. Preheat 10 minutes. Pour batter into the hot foil-lined pan and sprinkle with sugar. Bake, covered, for 20 minutes, or until a toothpick inserted in the center comes out clean. Serves 6 to 8.

At Home

Follow the above Dutch oven directions using a 10-inch cake pan. Bake at 325°F. for 20 minutes, or until toothpick inserted in the center comes out clean. Serves 6 to 8.

ORANGE PUDDING

1 (6-ounce) package instant vanilla pudding
4 cups milk
3 oranges, peeled, sectioned and sliced
Ice cream cones

In a small bowl, prepare pudding as directed on the package. (When camping, you can do this using a 1-gallon plastic self-sealing bag.)

Place on ice in the cooler or refrigerate until it thickens; stir in orange slices. Spoon into empty ice cream cones or dishes to serve. Serves 6 to 8.

• Set the plastic self-sealing bag in a 3-pound coffee can or #10-size can to serve.

PINEAPPLE UPSIDE-DOWN CAKE

This is my signature recipe. I have demonstrated it on television many times.

2 tablespoons butter or margarine, melted
1 (16-ounce) can pineapple slices, drained
1 (8-ounce) jar maraschino cherries
1/2 cup brown sugar
1 (18.25-ounce) box yellow cake mix, prepared
according to package directions

Dutch Oven

Line the bottom of a 12-inch Dutch oven with heavy-duty aluminum foil. Add butter or margarine and arrange pineapple slices on top. Set a maraschino cherry in the center of each pineapple slice, and sprinkle brown sugar evenly over the fruit. Pour prepared cake batter on top of the fruit.

Place the Dutch oven over 9 hot coals. Cover with Dutch oven lid and place 15 hot coals on the top. Bake, covered, for 30 minutes, or until golden brown and a toothpick inserted in the center comes out clean.

Lift the cake out of the Dutch oven using the aluminum foil lining and set it on the table. Cover the top with aluminum foil, and tuck the edges underneath the cake. Cool for 10 minutes; turn upside down and peel away the foil. Serves 10 to 12.

Dutch oven pineapple upside-down cake

At Home

Follow the above **Dutch oven** method using a cake pan lined with buttered parchment or waxed paper. Bake at 325°F. for 30 to 40 minutes, until golden brown and a toothpick inserted in the center comes out clean. Cool for 10 minutes. Turn upside down onto a platter and peel paper off.

• The pineapple juice can be substituted for the liquid in the cake mix directions.

POACHED AND STUFFED PEARS

2 tablespoons butter or margarine
1/4 cup brown sugar
2 (15-ounce) cans pear halves, drained (reserving 1/2 cup juice)
1 (4-ounce) package bleu cheese
1 cup walnuts, chopped
1/2 cup sour cream

Camp Stove and At Home

In a large skillet, add butter or margarine, sugar and reserved juice, and cook over high heat, stirring frequently, until sugar dissolves and a syrup forms. Turn down the heat and add pears, flat side down. Cook for 5 to 10 minutes, until pears are golden. Turn the pears over and fill with bleu cheese mixed with walnuts. Heat, covered, for 3 to 4 minutes, or until stuffing melts. Serve each pear in a small sauce dish with a small dollop of sour cream. Serves 6.

Dutch Oven

Heat a 12-inch Dutch oven over 12 hot coals; add butter or margarine, sugar and reserved juice, and cook, stirring frequently, until sugar dissolves and a syrup forms. Add the pears, flat side down, and cook for 5 to 10 minutes, until pears are golden. Turn the pears over and fill with bleu cheese mixed with walnuts. Heat, covered, 3 to 4 minutes, or until stuffing melts. Serve each pear in a sauce dish with a small dollop of sour cream.

• Substitute another semi-soft cheese if bleu cheese is not one of your favorites.

APPLE CRUNCH

This recipe is almost as good as apple pie and is a lot easier to make.

> **1/4 cup (1/2 stick) butter or margarine**
> **1/2 cup brown sugar**
> **1/4 teaspoon cinnamon**
> **1/4 teaspoon nutmeg**
> **6 cooking apples, peeled, cored and sliced**
> **2 cups sugar cookie crumbs**

Camp Stove and At Home

In a large skillet, melt butter and stir in sugar, cinnamon and nutmeg, and cook, stirring frequently, until sugar dissolves and a syrup forms. Cook apples in the syrup for 10 to 20 minutes, or until apples are soft. Top with cookie crumbs and serve hot or cold with **Kick-the-Can Ice Cream** (page 92). Serves 6.

Dutch Oven

Heat a 12-inch Dutch oven over 12 hot coals; melt butter and stir in sugar, cinnamon and nutmeg, and cook, stirring frequently, until sugar dissolves and a syrup forms. Cook apples in the syrup for 10 to 20 minutes, or until apples are soft. Top with cookie crumbs and serve hot or cold with **Kick-the-Can Ice Cream** (page 92). Serves 6.

• You may want to line the Dutch oven with heavy-duty aluminum foil before cooking for easy cleanup.

Appendix

ONE-DAY MEAL PLANNER

Breakfast

Protein Food

Cereal and/or bread

Fruit or juice

Other beverages

Utensils

Lunch

Main dish or salad

Vegetable and/or fruit

Bread

Dessert

Beverage

Utensils

Dinner

Main dish or salad

Vegetable and/or fruit

Bread

Dessert

Beverage

Utensils

Camping Equipment

The following is a checklist of camping equipment, cooking equipment and utensils, kitchen supplies and other miscellaneous equipment you can use as a guide for a camping trip.

Axe/hatchet/saw
Batteries (for flashlight)
Bucket
Bulbs (for flashlight)
Canteen
Clothesline and clothespins
Compass
Flashlight
Lantern (extra mantles and fuel)
Whistle

Packs
Rope (rappelling)
Ropes (small)
Shovel
String
Saw
Tent
Tin snips
Whetstone
Lashing twine
Maps
Wire

Cooking Equipment

Baking tins
Camp stove and fuel
Grill
Kettles
Muffin pan

Barbecuing equipment
Dutch oven
Heat-proof gloves
Mixing bowls
Reflector oven
Wire rack

Kitchen Tools

Can opener
Measuring equipment
Spatula
Toasting forks

Knives
Peeler
Spoons
Turners

Kitchen Supplies

Basic condiments and staples
Dishcloths and towels
Garbage bags
Lighter fluid
Matches
Napkins
Plates, cups, bowls
Silverware
Scrub pads
Storage containers
Charcoal briquettes
Foil
Hangers
Liquid soap
(biodegradable)
Newspapers
Paper towels
Plastic bags
Soap
Table cover

Clothing

Coat
Jacket, sweater or sweatshirt
Pajamas
Rain equipment
Shoes (two pair; one
for hiking)
Underclothing
Gloves
Hat
Pants (long)
Shirts
Socks (lightweight
and wool)

Sleeping Equipment

Ground cloth
Pillow
Insulated sleeping pad
Sleeping bags

Personal Items

Comb
Feminine hygiene products
Mirror
Toilet paper
Toothpaste
Insect repellent
Lip balm
Sunscreen
Toothbrush
Towel and washcloth

Miscellaneous

Camera and film
Medicine (Rx and over-
the-counter)
Sunglasses
First-aid kit
Musical instrument
Pocketknife

Camp Cooler—Care and Use

"Chilling out" in the outdoors is even easier with proper equipment. Camp coolers are available in sizes ranging from individual lunch-size to full-size versions on wheels. There are hard-side and soft-side varieties and many are designed specifically for backpacks, boats, RVs, etc. Beverage coolers, jugs, flasks and canteens come in many sizes for almost any drink imaginable.

Tips so you never lose your "cool" outdoors:

- Clean your cooler before and after each use with a soft cloth and a mild soap solution. Rinse well and allow to air dry before using or storing.
- Fill with ice at least 15 to 30 minutes before adding food or beverages.
- Freeze or prechill food and beverages to the proper temperature before adding to your cooler.
- Block ice will keep the contents cooler, longer than ice cubes. Blue ice packs are available for short-term use.
- You can make your own block ice by lining a #10-size can with a 1-gallon plastic self-sealing bag filled with water and freezing it overnight. Once the block begins to melt a little, you can remove the tin can for other uses at your campsite. Milk cartons also make good ice blocks.
- If your cooler has ice bottles or freezer flasks, you can fill them with your favorite noncarbonated beverage and enjoy a refreshing drink as they melt.
- Ice blocks can be placed in the bottom of the cooler, in the corners or on top of solid food items.
- Dry ice should be used only when heavily wrapped in several layers of newspaper. **Never allow dry ice to directly touch the surface of your cooler (or your skin).**
- Plan to pack the foods you will use first, such as breakfast, on the top. This avoids unnecessary opening of the cooler and keeps your food organized.

- Carefully store dry goods in the cooler tray or in plastic self-sealing bags to keep them from getting wet.
- For long trips you may want to use two coolers: one for *frozen* items (meats, frozen fruits or vegetables, juices or anything you won't be using right away); and the other cooler for *chilled* items (eggs, fresh vegetables, milk or anything you will be using right away). Small coolers for beverages are also convenient.
- Use a solution of chlorine bleach or vanilla extract to remove any unwanted odors from your cooler.
- Allow your cooler to air dry before storing and always store with the drain plug open.

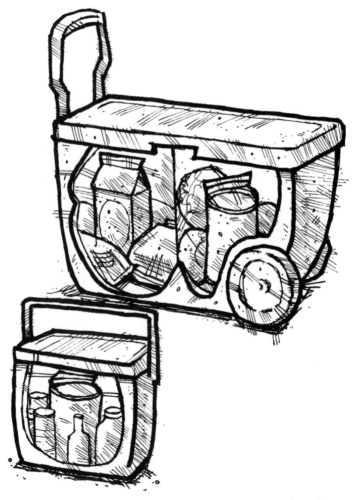

MARKET ORDER

PRODUCE	DAIRY	MEAT

FROZEN	CANNED	BAKERY

DRY GOODS	HOUSEHOLD SUPPLIES	MISC.

Index

Dian Thomas has fun for everyone!

Holiday Fun Year-Round

Dian Thomas' year-round collection of festive ideas and recipes will make every holiday special. You'll discover interesting tidbits of information about many holidays, why we observe them, and how to celebrate them with fun. You'll discover ideas for:

- A super Super Bowl party
- An exciting egg hunt for Easter
- Homemade gifts for Mother's Day and Father's Day
- Eerie decorations, creative costumes, and spooky treats for Halloween
- Creative Christmas ideas . . . and more. From New Year's to Christmas.

182 pages, full-color photos. **$19.99**

Fun at Home

This collection of creative ideas demonstrated on ABC's *Home Show* has something for everyone. Dian shows you how to keep the kids busy on a rainy day, make Kick-the-Can Ice Cream, and craft unique holiday decorations. It's a treasure of fun do-it-yourself or with-your-children projects! 200 pages with over 500 illustrations **$14.99**

ORDER TOLL FREE 1-800-846-6355
www.dianthomas.com

Recipes for Roughing It Easy

To properly equip the outdoor enthusiast, here are the best recipes for outdoor and campfire eating fun. From simply delicious breakfasts to "to-die-for" desserts, Dian Thomas shows readers how to cook inventive, flavorful meals in the great outdoors. Learn how to pack, prepare, and cook mouthwatering, easy-to-fix meals using portable gas stoves, aluminum foil, barbecue grills and Dutch ovens. With over 200 recipes and 145 photos, this is a book novices will appreciate, with tips on packing food for camping, creating a portable pantry, directions for preparing scrumptious meals, or making intended leftovers. Experienced campers will relish Dian's favorite ideas for novelty cooking—such as cooking chicken in a backpack while hiking, frying eggs and bacon in a paper bag, and even making ice cream in the woods! 240 pages. **$14.99**

Roughing It Easy

Even the camp cooks have fun when they're *Roughing It Easy!* This New York Times best-seller is chock-full of recipes and great ideas that make outdoor camping and cooking an adventure. It is the complete camper's bible. Cook eggs and bacon in a paper cup, and start a fire with steel wool and batteries! There are suggestions for equipment selection, fire building, campfire cooking, solar cooking, and even drying your own foods for backpacking! If you love the out-of-doors, *Roughing It Easy* is for you! In this new, expanded edition, Dian will also teach you about emergency planning for home, family and auto; and 72-hour kits and 30-day emergency supplies. 272 pages. **$14.99**

Backyard Roughing It Easy

Backyard Roughing It Easy is synonymous with fun! In this book, Dian takes you on an outdoor adventure with her creative ideas for family fun. Dian answers all of your questions from how to start a fire to the do's and don'ts of planning a backyard camping trip with your family. Don't have a grill? Why not turn an ash can into a newspaper stove? Need tips for easy outdoor entertaining? Look no further; Dian's recipes and party ideas will make you the talk of the town. *Backyard Roughing It Easy* is filled to the brim with innovative, yet practical, tips for outdoor living. You'll never look at your backyard the same way again. 180 pages. **$14.99**

Dutch Oven Cooking Basics

Dian Thomas, an avid Dutch oven cook, is your guide to learning everything you need to know about getting started with Dutch oven cooking. She walks you step-by-step as she energetically prepares delicious recipes and shows unique ways to use your oven. VHS 30 min. **$9.99**

Dian has more ideas online! Log on to www.dianthomas.com and see the most creative spot in cyberspace.

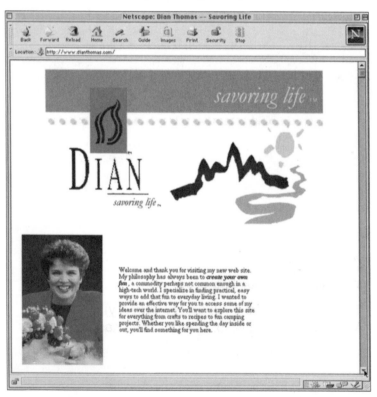

ORDER TOLL FREE 1-800-846-6355
www.dianthomas.com

It's Easy to Order More Fun *from* Dian Thomas!

Order by mail or call toll free 1-800-846-6355

Name _____

Address _____

City/State/ZIP _____

Telephone (_____) _____

email _____

DESCRIPTION	QTY	UNIT PRICE	TOTAL
Holiday Fun Year-Round		19.99	
Fun at Home		14.99	
Recipes for Roughing It Easy		14.99	
Roughing It Easy		14.99	
Backyard Roughing It Easy		14.99	
Dutch Oven Cooking Basics video		9.99	

*Add $3.00 shipping/handling for first item and $1.00 for each additional item.

•Canadian residents add 30% to total.

SUBTOTAL $ _____

SHIPPING AND HANDLING* $ _____

UTAH RESIDENTS ADD 6.7% SALES TAX $ _____

TOTAL $ _____

Send with payment or credit card information to:
The Dian Thomas Company, PO Box 171107, Holladay, UT 84117
or call toll free 1-800-846-6355

☐ Check/Money Order (please, no currency)
  Make checks payable to: **The Dian Thomas Co.**

☐ Visa ☐ MasterCard ☐ Discover ☐ American Express
Card Number _____
(Please list all numbers on card)

Signature _____ Exp. Date _____

Thank you for your order